Other books by Julie King:

*Arise My Darling: Encounters with Jesus to Ignite Passion, Worship, and Wonder*

*Revivalist Arise: Encounters with Jesus that Position You to Carry the Fires of Revival*

# Arise and Go

## The Harvest Has Come

### A 40-Day Journey Into Pursuing the Great Commission

JULIE KING

Arise and Go!
The Harvest Has Come
A 40-Day Journey Into Pursuing the Great Commission

Julie King | East-West



To contact the author: julie.king@eastwest.org

For updated information on events, trips, resources, and ways to get involved, visit our website at www.eastwest.org/arise.

ISBN (Print): 978-1-7374997-7-0
ISBN (E-book): 978-1-7374997-8-7

Published by
East-West
Plano, TX

# Dedication

I dedicate this book to my mom and dad, Doug and Evaleen Harris, who brought me the salvation of Jesus at a very young age. They raised my brother and me to live a life of radical faith and deposited in our DNA what it means to follow Jesus no matter the cost. I am grateful for their legacy of faithful obedience and unwavering faith. My life pursuits of Jesus and the world He died for is directly tied to the legacy of my mom and dad, to which I will honor all my days.

Special thanks to the women in the Arise movement who are raising their hands to be missionaries to our nation and the nations. This is the most redemptive thing we can do in this hour. Thank you for living a life that is set apart for the glory of God and the salvation of nations.

Thank you to my mission trip co-leaders (you know who you are) for helping me get teams of women into the field to bring the power and presence of Jesus. I can't wait to celebrate with you for all eternity as we see all those who have come to faith because you were willing to leave families and jobs and comforts to go to the most unreached areas to bring the good news of Jesus!

# Contents

# Foreword

When I think of Julie King, the word passion comes to mind as a singular definition of her heart, mind, soul, spirit, and the way she lives every moment of her life. When we use passion in a formal sense, as in The Passion, we are referring to the suffering and death of Jesus, the Son of God, the King of Kings, and the Lord of Lords. Jesus is the focal passion of Julie's life and mission, and therefore not surprisingly, of her writing as well.

The primary application of her passion is to see women encounter Jesus as never before and, in complete surrender to His love and lordship over their lives, totally surrendering to His calling upon their lives. Julie is merely asking you to do what she does every day of her life: to say, "Yes," to Jesus' calling upon your life by denying yourself, surrendering to Him, being filled afresh with His Holy Spirit, and going forth in His power and anointing to do mighty exploits for His Kingdom and for His glory alone.

You are in for a true blessing over the next 40 days as you read God's Word, hear Julie's heart, worship God in songs and hymns and spiritual songs, and read supernatural testimonies of the healing power of the gospel and the Holy Spirit. My prayer (and Julie's) is that you will encounter God as Father, Son, and Spirit as never before in your life, and will arise and go for your own good and for God's great glory! Arise, dear sisters! Be blessed!

*"The Lord announces the word, and the women who proclaim it* ***are a mighty throng*** *... ."*
*-Psalm 68:11*

Kurt Nelson
President and CEO, East-West

"The time is now! There is an **urgency** by the Spirit of Grace to lay the sickle into the ripened harvest fields now and without delay." -Patricia King, emphasis added

# Introduction

*"'Very truly I tell you, whoever believes in me will do the works I have been doing, and they will do even greater things than these, because I am going to the Father.'" -John 14:12*

*"These were all commended for their faith, yet none of them received what had been promised, since God had planned something better for us so that only together with us would they be made perfect." -Hebrews 11:39-40*

*"'However, I consider my life worth nothing to me; my only aim is to finish the race and complete the task the Lord Jesus has given me—the task of testifying to the good news of God's grace.'" -Acts 20:24*

*"'But you will receive power when the Holy Spirit comes on you; and you will be my witnesses in Jerusalem, and in all Judea and Samaria, and to the ends of the earth.'" -Acts 1:8*

*"'Look, I am coming soon! My reward is with me, and I will give to each person according to what they have done.'" -Revelation 22:12*

I recently returned from a powerful and gut-wrenching trip to Latin America where our team of nine ministered in a nation decimated by years of communism. They endured the COVID-19 lockdowns with no medicine, unclean water, and food shortages. Many people are fleeing this country because they cannot endure the suffering any longer. Many believers are falling away in the midst of the pain. We sat with them in their homes, and hundreds and hundreds of people gave their lives to Jesus. My team returned with their hearts wrecked for the lost. This was not a one-time event for these nine; it was the beginning of a life centered on the Great Commission. Many people will go on an evangelism trip and place a period at the end of that week. Their hearts are moved, but they go back to life as normal. Not these nine. This trip ended with an ellipsis as they asked the Lord for what is next for each of them and remained simply undone in His goodness.

I know my calling. It's not only to be a missionary to my nation and the nations, but it is to raise up other women who are shifting their lives from pursuing the great American dream to pursuing the Great Commission. I am looking for women who want to raise their hands and say, "Whatever it costs, Jesus, send me." To raise up missionaries in our nation is one of the most redemptive moves of the Spirit I can do as we watch America quickly slip into post-Christendom. We used to be the number one sending nation of missionaries since the birth of our nation, but no longer is that the reality. I long to answer the promise of God's heart in Psalm 68:11, *"The Lord announces the word, and the women who proclaim it* ***are a mighty throng...*** *(emphasis added)."*

We are in an Acts 29 chapter, where the story is being written by surrendered lives who are answering the call of the Spirit and following Jesus no matter the cost. We are also living in a place where the Church has been lulled asleep, and the Great Commission is passed to a select few. Jesus never intended the Great Commission to become "the Great Suggestion." How did we even get to this place in America?

The assignments and callings we have been entrusted to fulfill are specifically for the present-day Church. We have been assigned a responsibility to finish the missionary task not given to any other generation. Our assignments are given on the heels of those who have gone before us, who have poured their lives out for the gospel, who have sown the ground in tears and intercession, and who have worked the harvest field faithfully. **The current revival we are in today has come because of the faithfulness of the Lord to His Word and the faithful harvesters who went ahead of us in both prayer and movement**. And looking on is the great cloud of witnesses, cheering and praying for us to finish our race.

> "People were attracted to the early church. Who wouldn't be fascinated by a group that shared possessions, rejoiced nonstop, had peace beyond comprehension and immeasurable power, never complained, always gave thanks ...? Some people joined them, others hated them, but few could ignore them. They wouldn't allow people to ignore them as they went out fearlessly sharing the gospel. This is our heritage. This is in our DNA. We must stop creating safe places for people to hide and start developing fearless warriors to send out." -Francis Chan, "Letters to the Church"[1]

Here's the grave reality for many people today: Jesus is coming back, and they do not know Him. We have been entrusted to preach the gospel of God's grace to the ends of the Earth. We take only one thing with us to Heaven—other people. We can't take our barns full of cash investments or our homes stashed full of our earthly treasures. Beloved in the Lord, this is our hour of rerouting to get our eyes focused on Christ, who is standing at the finish line. It requires a level of surrender and sanctification that only Jesus can do in us. But this is the life and the ellipsis of the Christ follower: *"For to me, to live is Christ ... (Philippians 1:21)."* He fills in the rest.

We have the joy of fulfilling the assignments and callings of past generations. What they started we carry to completion. But we can also abort our own callings and obedience because of distraction, idols of the heart, weariness, and lack of repentance. Let it not be said of us who are awakening to the Spirit of God in a bold and courageous way that **we ever discarded the call of God**. I pray that each one of us will stay awake, stay anchored in the Word of God, and not fall away when scores of saints soon lose their theological footing (it's already beginning to take place). It's imperative to finish this last lap, holding on to Jesus with everything we've got.

"We have come to that place in history now, and the Lord looks to us ... . Will we be His people now, as the world looks to us in the midst of madness? Our Bible studies and sermons have all been meaningless if we do not make what we learned come alive in ways that are self-sacrificial and that show that we really do know that God has defeated death. To do anything less than this is to represent a lie, and to lie to God in doing so. How else shall we put it? This is the hour for which each of us has been born. If we live fully in that freedom for which Christ has set us free, we will see God's hand in ways we dare not imagine. We will see miracles small and great, and we will see not only revival, but reformation. We will see the goodness of God make its way into everything we do, because that is God's will for us and for the world at this time." -Eric Metaxas, "Letter to the American Church"[2]

This book contains 40 devotionals. In the Bible, the number 40 represents spiritual preparation for assignments that are to come. Remember the stories of Moses in the wilderness, Jesus being tempted, the flood? This devotional will prepare you for what God has in store for you next. He is calling you to step into the harvest field with Him. Just as He led Moses, He will lead you. At the end of each devotional, I have included a testimony from people who have traveled with me into the mission field. Though the testimonies do not directly relate to the devotionals, they do give an account of how God works, moves, and glorifies His name when we step out in faith to take Jesus to those who do not yet know Him.

God, please have mercy on Your people and give us the grace to stay awake and fulfill what was on Your heart when You commissioned each of us in Matthew 28:18-20, *"Then Jesus came to them and said, 'All authority in heaven and on earth has been given to me. Therefore go and make disciples of all nations, baptizing them in the name of the Father and of the Son and of the Holy Spirit, and teaching them to obey everything I have commanded you. And surely I am with you always, to the very end of the age.*'" Find us faithful with our lamps filled with oil when You return. Jesus, help us not to become sleepy, fearful, and distracted in this hour. Guard us by Your mercy and grace.

I will meet you in the harvest field!

# TESTIMONY
## Open Doors in Latin America

While in the Caribbean on a mission trip, we went with our church worker to share the gospel, going from home to home. After being turned away numerous times, I asked God to miraculously open doors for us so we could tell others about Him. As we walked by a home, a young woman with two small children came onto her porch. Our church worker asked if we could come into her home and share with her. As we talked, the young woman shared that she knew Jesus as a child but had walked away and not followed Him for years. As I shared with her, she recommitted her life to Christ. Afterward, she asked how we knew her name to call out as we were walking by. She was shocked when I told her we didn't know her name before coming to her house. The reason she came onto the porch was because she heard someone calling her name. I know it was Jesus calling her outside to meet us so we could share the good news with her and bring her back to Him. Praise God, for He knows His sheep and calls them each by name.

Becky

# DAY 1

## What Do You Want?

*"The next day John was there again with two of his disciples. When he saw Jesus passing by, he said, 'Look, the Lamb of God!'*

*"When the two disciples heard him say this, they followed Jesus. Turning around, Jesus saw them following and asked, '**What do you want?**'*

*"They said, 'Rabbi' (which means 'Teacher'), 'where are you staying?'*

*"'**Come,**' he replied, '**and you will see.**'*

*"So they went and saw where he was staying, and they spent that day with him. It was about four in the afternoon. Andrew, Simon Peter's brother, was one of the two who heard what John had said and who had followed Jesus. The first thing Andrew did was to find his brother Simon and tell him, 'We have found the Messiah' (that is, the Christ). And he brought him to Jesus. Jesus looked at him and said, 'You are Simon son of John. You will be called Cephas' (which, when translated, is Peter). The next day Jesus decided to leave for Galilee. Finding Philip, he said to him, '**Follow me.**'" -John 1:35-43, emphasis added*

Today begins a 40-day, intimate journey about knowing Jesus and being known by Him. We will look at His face as He looks at us. We will look at His face when He encounters His disciples and calls them to go with Him on His journey to and beyond the cross. I pray that our encounters over the next 40 days will mark us forever. Jesus invites us to come and attentively behold Him—to fix our gaze upon Him.

Jesus steps onto the scene, and all of history changes forever, beginning with a select few. The living Word, who existed before the very beginning, came to bring hope and salvation to all humankind, and He's not stopping now. The first disciples behold the Son of God, and Jesus asks them, "What do you want?" Can you see His look of eager longing and joy?

"What do you want?" Leaning in, He is asking this of you, eye to eye and heart to heart. He asked a probing question that He asks us today at the start of these 40 days. What do we want from Jesus? What do you need from Him? How do you long for Him to reveal Himself in deeper ways? Jesus leans in and wants to hear you pour out your longings and desires before Him. His eyes are transfixed on you, waiting for your answer.

"Want" is derived from the Greek verb meaning to seek, strive for, desire, enquire, to crave. What begins as curiosity in the life of a believer ends in craving. Wherever you find yourself on this journey, may it end in an insatiable craving for the One who is gazing at you with a depth of love that changes everything. Do you equally crave His intimacy as He does with you?

*"And let us all advance together to reach this victory-prize, following one path with one passion." -Philippians 3:16, TPT*

As you have expressed your heart to Jesus in all your wanting, He now invites you on an adventure: Come and see! Come and see how He is going to answer these longings, desires, and expectations. Come and see how you are going to begin to crave Him as you spend time with Him in intentional and intimate pursuit.

To "see" in the Greek sense is quite comprehensive. It means to see with the eyes, to know or perceive with the mind, and to become acquainted with by experience. It's to behold, perceive, and take heed. Jesus had so much expectation when He invited these first ones to take a step and let their entire sight, understanding, and experience be shifted by their Savior.

His invitation to them resembles the one for us today: Come and see! Come and behold Jesus. Gaze upon His beautiful face when He called the first disciples with anticipation for all that was ahead for them. He knew the invitation to a life following Him would not only transform them but ultimately the entire world. To move in closer would require both their faith and their feet. They couldn't stand at a distance and engage intimately. They had to come in closer. It was both a decision of their will and an act of faith.

Then He invites them to a life characterized by possibility and the unknown! *"'Follow me.'"*

> "Jesus' disciples did not all look alike. They didn't have identical resumes. What was it about these men, and soon to come women and even children, that elicited a 'Follow Me' from Jesus? Was it their pedigree, their influence, their status in the community … or was it their heart? Was this what Jesus saw?" -Mary Jo Pierce, "Follow Me: An Unending Conversation with Jesus"[3]

What destiny does He have for you when He says to you, "Follow Me"? It's critical at this time in history that we know our calling and we know our finish line: Christ Himself. There is a world at stake needing passionate Christ followers to know this at a bone-deep level. The Great Commission hinges on your seeing Jesus and clearly knowing your calling.

> "Do you know where the hope for your city is? It's sitting in your chair right now. God's plan of revival for your city is you—Him working in and through you. There's no need to wait for something else to come. You've come. And because you've come, Christ has shown up. I pray that you believe that. I pray that you grab hold of God's promises for you. Christ came to save and to seek what was lost and to destroy the works of the enemy. Because

> taking his power and presence to the streets is important to Him, it's got to be important to you and to me." -Robby Dawkins, "Do What Jesus Did"[4]

We find our identity in the knowing of His love, and we also find our destiny. He's invited you to take 40 days and press into **who** He is and **what** is ahead for you. These days are going to be both introspective and eternity-focused. Time is short, and Jesus is coming back. We are getting our lamps filled with oil, our wicks trimmed, and our gaze focused. The finish line is in sight, so let's run to Jesus unhindered, overflowing, and established in the love Christ has for us. Enjoy Him; He's worth everything you sacrifice and every voice of worship you offer Him.

Listen to this worship song: "He Made Me, He Loves Me" by Ben & Noelle Kilgore

# TESTIMONY
## What Do You Want?

Our son, Doug, was 16 years old when he became very sick. The doctor told us that Doug had Epstein-Barr virus, better known as "the kissing disease." Doug had swollen lymph glands and an enlarged spleen, and the doctor said it would take several weeks for him to recover. While Doug was resting, I walked into his bedroom and asked, "What do you want? Do you want God to heal you?" He answered, "Yes." By faith, I said a simple prayer asking God to heal him in the name of Jesus. The next day, Doug went surfing and the virus never returned. Jesus is our Healer and the Great Physician. He is faithful. All we need to do is ask.

Ev

# It's Go Time!

*"Now, beloved brothers and sisters, concerning the question of God's precise times and specific seasons, you don't need me to write anything to you. For you already know quite well that the day of the Lord will come unexpectedly and as a complete surprise. For while some are saying, 'Finally we have peace and security,' sudden destruction will arrive at their doorstep, like labor pains seizing a pregnant woman—and with no chance of escape! But you, beloved brothers and sisters, are not living in the dark, allowing that day to creep up on you like a thief coming to steal.* ***For you are all children of the light and children of the day****. We don't belong to the night nor to darkness.* ***This is why we must not fall asleep, as the rest do, but keep wide awake and clearheaded.*** *For those who are asleep sleep the night away, and drunkards get drunk at night.* ***But since we belong to the day, we must stay alert and clearheaded by placing the breastplate of faith and love over our hearts, and a helmet of the hope of salvation over our thoughts****. For God has not destined us for wrath* ***but to possess salvation*** *through our Lord Jesus, the Anointed One.* ***He gave his life for us so that we may share in resurrection life in union with him****—whether we're awake or asleep. Because of this, encourage the hearts of your fellow believers and support one another, just as you have already been doing."*

*-1 Thessalonians 5:1-11, TPT, emphasis added*

Daughters of the light, my spirit is welling up inside of me with these words: **"It's go time!"** We have a season ahead that we have never had before, nor will we ever have again. We have an open window of opportunity to seize with faith and courage while it is still **day**. This will be a key year for many of God's people as He takes us not only to the deeper place in His heart for the lost but to a more narrowing consecration and circumcision of our own hearts. This won't come with an easy path because the path He is asking you to walk is narrow, and only the righteous walk on it. It requires hard choices, cooperation with His sanctification, and a willingness to lose your life for the sake of Christ. But if we are going to be found being about His work when He returns, it's time to get out of bed, awaken, and run the race set before you.

I love what my friend Patrice Vines said to me. She told the Lord, "When You return, I want You to find me busy about Your work." I want the Lord to find me right in the middle of the harvest field, preaching the gospel and confirming it with miracles, signs, and wonders. It's **go** time!

*"The one who calls you is faithful, and he will do it."*
*-1 Thessalonians 5:24*

Our submission to His leadership and to the sanctification of our lives is an invitation based on mercy and grace and love. He will do it. We position ourselves in dependence, and He will do it!

Awake, sober, and watchful—this was the exhortation that Paul had for the Thessalonians. He taught them to be wide-awake and not metaphorically in bed with the covers over their heads, waiting for the storm to pass. He taught them what to look for in the return of Jesus. They needed to be mindful and aware of the times and seasons in which they were living because the end was near. (It's nearer now than it even was then!) He was encouraging them, however, to live with wide-awake sobriety so that they would be about the work of the Lord, not consumed with the darkness that surrounded them (times) nor the culture (seasons) that sought to entrap them. Were they ready for the day of the Lord? They could be totally prepared for the unexpected—the day when He will come for His own!

> "In some respect, the coming of Jesus will be a surprise for *everybody*, because no one knows the day or the hour (Matthew 24:36). But for Christians who know the *times and the seasons*, it will not be a complete surprise. No one knows the exact hour a thief will come, but some live in a general preparation against thieves. Those **who are not in darkness**, who live as they **are all sons of light and sons of the day**, these are ready for the return of Jesus. But if we *are* **in darkness**—perhaps caught up in some of the sin Paul warned against previously in this letter—then we are *not* ready and need to make ourselves ready for the return of Jesus." -David Guzik, 1 Thessalonians 5 commentary[5]

Are you ready to get ready? This is where we avail ourselves of the counsel of the Holy Spirit. He has been speaking things to me that are areas He wants to sanctify and strengthen. His counsel will never come with shame or condemnation but rather invitation and grace.

*"So then, let us not be like others, who are asleep,*
*but let us be awake and sober."*
*-1 Thessalonians 5:6*

"Awake" is defined by Merriam-Webster as "Fully conscious, alert, and aware: not asleep." This is to be our spiritual condition. And if it is not, we must ask the Lord to declare to our body, soul, and spirit, "Awake! Awake!" (Pray these words right now if you need them!)

> "The word *sleep* is here used metaphorically to denote indifference to spiritual realities on the part of believers. It is a different word than that in 4:13-15 for the sleep of death. It covers all sorts of moral and spiritual laxity or insensibility." -Edmond Hiebert

"Sober" is defined by Merriam-Webster as "Sparing in the use of food and drink; marked by sedate or gravely or earnestly thoughtful character or demeanor."

Sobriety isn't a passionless life, lacking zeal and enthusiasm; it's a life lived with intentionality and focus. It's one who has learned to tame the flesh and live in the overflow of the Spirit. The one filled with the Holy Spirit is both intoxicated and passionately in love with Jesus. The sober-minded believer has only the things of Christ to pursue and a lost world to go to and bring to salvation. The external intoxications such as food and drink and earthly pleasures grow more and more dim in His presence and glorious grace.

Paul emphasizes getting that breastplate and helmet back in place as we finish our race. Our union with Christ is our positional authority for the days in which we are living. In light of that, we each have some work to do as we prepare for two things: the return of Christ and the massive end-time harvest that is now upon us.

Therefore:

*"May God himself, the God of peace, sanctify you through and through. May your whole spirit, soul and body be kept blameless at the coming of our Lord Jesus Christ. The one who calls you is faithful,* ***and he will do it****."*
*-1 Thessalonians 5:23-24, emphasis added*

As part of the sanctification process of walking in humility and truth, we ask the Lord to search us and know us. And as He does, we come back into agreement with His truth and what He says about us (repentance). The turning of our eyes and hearts before Him is critical as we prepare.

- Repent of anything done in darkness. He's calling you back to living in the light.
- Repent of pride. Humility is our only way forward.
- Repent of sleepiness. He's calling to His Bride, "Awake, awake!"

- Repent of drunkenness. He's wanting to intoxicate you with Himself.
- Repent of being OK with living in darkness. This world is no longer your home.
- Repent of justifying a lack of self-control. Make room for the fruit of His Spirit, not the fruit of your flesh.
- Repent of taking off faith, love, and self-control. It's time to have Him dress you again.
- Repent of forsaking your union with Him in a prayerless life. Let's run back to the secret place with Him.

It's imperative to awaken, come alive, and throw off the things that are entangling and tripping us up. It's time to go with Jesus His way. I received a text from my dear friend who wrote, "I'm praying the Lord continues to make both of us uncomfortable so we can grow and mature for the days that truly matter—the days that will require **seasoned** lovers of the Lord to stand. He is readying us for the days when we need leaders with grit and clarity." Amen to this prayer. Let it be said of you and me.

I close with this prayer for us:

> Awaken us, Lord, from the top of our heads to the soles of our feet that we would chase our Lover into the harvest field and live the rest of our days on Your agenda and Your plan. Give us grit and zeal and passion and sobriety and watchfulness until You return. Teach us the times and seasons in which we are living so that intentionality and a heart of wisdom mark our **every** day. May we be found knee-deep in Your business when You return, overwhelmed by the light of Your presence and not hiding in darkness. Pour out Your Spirit on us, in Jesus' powerful and merciful name! Maranatha, come, Lord Jesus, come!

Listen to this worship song: "Surrendered" by One House Worship

# TESTIMONY
## Raised Up to Follow Christ

I was not looking to go on a mission trip, but after being invited, I sensed the Lord say, *"For whoever wants to save their life will lose it … (Matthew 16:24)."* I began to pray that God would swing wide the gates of people's hearts, homes, and Latin America, where we were going. I had never done a trip like this, and I kept thinking, "I don't want to miss what God is doing." By His grace, I was privileged to pray with more than 60 people of all ages to receive the Lord.

One day, we visited a home where there were multiple generations of girls and women. We shared the gospel while we sat outside. All of the girls and women prayed to receive Christ, and the youngest, Melanie, asked if she could come with us as we continued to visit homes and share Jesus. She was 10 years old, although she looked much younger because she was small and thin. She carried my bag and proceeded to walk with us to other houses.

Melanie heard the gospel multiple times that day, and I thought, "She's the next missionary!" At one home, I again shared the gospel with a group of girls and women. As I finished, a group of eager boys ran up, so I shared again. They all prayed, and it was a beautiful site.

The pastor's wife, Julie, was my church worker that day. They had just planted a church in that village, and at the end of the day, she said, "I think we'll start with a children's ministry because of the contacts made today!" It warmed my heart to see the next generation being raised up to follow Christ. I was able to tell them, "I met Jesus when I was 9, and He's been with me through every difficulty and joy in life, and He will never leave you. This is the most important decision of your life!" My translator, Richard, said again and again, "Susan, God sent you here!"

Susan

# DAY 3

# Awaken Your Bride

*"So the word of God spread. The number of disciples in Jerusalem increased rapidly, and a large number of priests became obedient to the faith.*

*"Now Stephen, a man full of God's grace and power, performed great wonders and signs among the people. Opposition arose, however, from members of the Synagogue of the Freedmen (as it was called)—Jews of Cyrene and Alexandria as well as the provinces of Cilicia and Asia—who began to argue with Stephen. But they could not stand up against* ***the wisdom the Spirit gave him*** *as he spoke." -Acts 6:7–10, emphasis added*

*"When they heard these things, they were overtaken with violent rage filling their souls, and they gnashed their teeth at him. But Stephen,* ***overtaken with great faith,*** *was* ***full of the Holy Spirit.*** *He* ***fixed his gaze*** *into the heavenly realm and saw the glory and splendor of God—and Jesus, who stood up at the right hand of God. 'Look!' Stephen said. 'I can see the heavens opening and the Son of Man standing at the right hand of God to welcome me home!'*

*"His accusers covered their ears with their hands and screamed at the top of their lungs to drown out his voice. Then they pounced on him and threw him outside the city walls to stone him. His accusers, one by one, placed their outer garments at the feet of a young man named Saul of Tarsus. As they hurled stone after stone at him, Stephen prayed, 'Our Lord Jesus, accept my spirit into your presence.' He crumpled to his*

*knees and shouted in a loud voice, 'Our Lord, don't hold this sin against them.' And then he died." -Acts 7:54–59, TPT, emphasis added*

There are so many poignant moments in scripture, but this moment has been lingering in my spirit. It was a really important moment to Jesus, and I believe He suffered with Stephen. Stephen also entered into the sufferings of Christ. His beloved Stephen was significant to the explosive growth of the Church both by his life and by his death. I remember walking through the place in Israel believed to be where Stephen was stoned, and I was overwhelmed with emotion. Stephen didn't deserve to die, but Jesus opened Heaven and allowed him to see his Lord in order to persevere till the very end. The death of Jesus' saints means so much to Him (Psalm 116:15). He knows what it costs on every level.

**We must have a vision of Jesus if we are going to persevere to the very end.**

His love never fails. It didn't fail in the death of this Spirit-filled man of God. It didn't fail in all those loved ones we have lost. His love never fails. The injustice created by persecution and murder matters deeply to the Lord. We must know His heart of compassion toward our suffering. We must be able to look at His face to strengthen us in moments far beyond our capacity to endure. He is not far off, and in fact, was so present that He stood to welcome home Stephen—who is considered the first martyr of the Christian faith.

Stephen was so filled with the Holy Spirit, that his face shone like that of an angel (Acts 6:15). Even in death, his response was the very words Jesus spoke on the cross. He was longing for his enemies' forgiveness more than his own justice. He fixed his gaze on Jesus, and his words pierced the religious ones who knew nothing about the grace or the love of Christ.

Saul (who became Paul) was marked all of his days by Stephen's martyrdom. In fact, it was Stephen's request for forgiveness that God used on behalf of Paul to launch the ministry of this pillar of Christianity. Saint Augustine said, "If Stephen had not prayed, the church would not have had Paul." That's profound to me—to realize the power of our forgiveness in the lives of others.

The wisdom and truth in his words caused them to violently respond. The religious felt quite justified in their own minds about the stoning of this man. Their convictions moved them not toward repentance and grace but toward anger and rage. Conviction will compel us to the grace of Jesus or toward the justification required by the law.

> "He takes the sharp knife of the Word and rips up the sins of the people, laying open the inward parts of their hearts, and the secrets of their soul … . He could not have delivered that searching address with greater fearlessness had he been assured that they would thank him for the operation; the fact that his death was certain had no other effect upon him than to make him yet more zealous." -Charles Spurgeon

Although I could write a whole book on bondage from religion, the greater spotlight in this segment of the story is the power of the Holy Spirit to accomplish much through Stephen's life. I like J.B. Phillips' translation: *"Stephen, filled through all his being with the Holy Spirit … (Acts 7:55)."*

- He spoke the word boldly and with deep immovable conviction in the power of the Spirit.
- He did not preserve his life over the truth of the saving grace of Jesus by the power of the Spirit.
- He spoke with wisdom by the power of the Spirit.
- His gaze and hope were fixed on Jesus by the power of the Spirit.
- He was overcome with faith by the power of the Spirit.
- He was overcome with forgiveness by the power of the Spirit.
- He did not shrink from death, for the sake of Christ, by the power of the Spirit.

- He trusted in Christ, against all odds, by the power of the Spirit.
- He died in dignity by the power of the Spirit, with a standing ovation from Heaven.

Stephen was a mere man who was filled through and through by the power of the Spirit. It defined his very life and his very death! How greatly we can partner with the Lord as we walk in the power of the Spirit of God who dwells in us.

> "The fires ... in the olden days never made martyrs; they revealed them. No hurricane of persecution ever creates martyrs; it reveals them. Stephen was a martyr before they stoned him. He was the first martyr to seal his testimony with his blood." -G. Campbell Morgan

In the New International Version translation, it uses the term *"he fell asleep (Acts 7:60)."* This is what happens to believers—we pass from one life to the next (1 Thessalonians 4:13–18). But catch the catalytic spark of this! **When Stephen fell asleep, the Church had to wake up!** The blood of this martyr sent ripple effects through the believers, and the spiritual ground beneath them began to shake the nest where they hid. Just like how the blood of Jesus being poured out for us shook the ground, tore the temple curtain, raised the dead, and made a way back for us to the Father. So, the believers were being moved into their own awakening.

It's our turn now as we look at His face these 40 days. This is our hour of awakening as the beloved in Christ. Just like Stephen, we are overflowing with the Spirit of God who dwells in us. Our very countenance, perspective, vision, and expression of the power of God are able to be sanctified and manifested. We can live and respond like Stephen in the face of our accusers, not bound by fear of man or fear of death. We get to live differently from religiously bound people. We are overcomers, even unto death. We have the power of forgiveness, mercy, grace, and love to give away as a tidal wave over our enemies and those who persecute us. Our forgiveness can propel others into their mission! Jesus, help us to understand the power of Christ in us in this hour!

> "God is raising up an army of lovers who will go anywhere and do anything for Him." -Jennifer Miskov, "Fasting for Fire"[6]
>
> "The problem is not the lack of a power supply in heaven, but the supply of faithful workers willing to go out and speak out in risk." -Robby Dawkins, "Do What Jesus Did"[7]
>
> Lord Jesus, awaken us! Awaken your Bride! Let us be the wide-awake army of lovers who move in power and speak with courage and fearlessness. I pray for all the women reading these words that You would ignite us and move us to the front lines of this great movement of God to bring the Kingdom of Heaven to Earth!

Listen to this worship song: "The One You Love" by Elevation Worship

# TESTIMONY
## Journey to Freedom

My mom was neglected by her alcoholic mom and became pregnant with me at 15 years old. An alcoholic at 16, unwed and desperate, she worked during the day at a grocery store and at night as a waitress. She started using drugs to help her stay awake for her second job. While she worked and partied, she left me in various places with various people, which led to mental, physical, and sexual abuse during my childhood. As I entered my teen years, I started having bad dreams, reliving the real-life nightmares my brain had blocked to protect me. To dull the pain, I started using alcohol and drugs. My mom finally met and married a good man, but she continued to abuse alcohol.

We moved a few times to get away from bad influences and have a fresh start. But as I grew older, I attempted suicide several times and increased my drug use to further dull the pain. Knowing I wasn't going to survive without help, I started counseling to try to break free from the past. I continued to drink and, periodically, would have an episode of over-drinking and blacking out. Wearing many masks and trying to be a good person, wife, and mother, I was exhausted and started developing health problems from carrying around so much baggage.

In March 2013, God impressed on me that I was about to throw away all the blessings and answers to my childhood dreams—my beautiful family. I finally listened to Him and sought an initiative outpatient program, deciding to do whatever it took to stop drinking. The first month was hard because I didn't realize the extent of my addiction and my need for God's help. He brought amazing people to encourage, pray, and lead me down a path I never dreamt was possible. I received inner healing, deliverance, and breakthroughs that completely transformed me. Today, I walk in freedom from addiction and in joy.

Because God did such an amazing work in me and led me into a place of deep healing and forgiveness, I was able to forgive my mom and help her see God's love for her. Then God had me pray for generational healing. All of this led to another miracle! My mom woke up one morning free from cigarette and alcohol addiction too! She never got help or entered any program. She desired to be free but didn't think it would be possible. Now, she's transformed, too! With God, anything is possible!

Shannon

# Sister, Get Up!

*"When the disciples heard this, they fell facedown to the ground, terrified. But Jesus came and touched them. '**Get up**,' he said. 'Don't be afraid.' When they looked up, they saw no one except Jesus."*
*-Matthew 17:6-8, emphasis added*

*"'I tell you, **get up**, take your mat and go home.'"*
*-Mark 2:11, emphasis added*

*"He took her by the hand and said to her, 'Talitha koum!' (which means 'Little girl, I say to you, **get up**!')."*
*-Mark 5:41, emphasis added*

*"Then he went up and touched the bier they were carrying him on, and the bearers stood still. He said, 'Young man, I say to you, **get up!**'"*
*-Luke 7:14, emphasis added*

*"But he took her by the hand and said, 'My child, **get up**!'"*
*-Luke 8:54, emphasis added*

*"'Aeneas,' Peter said to him, 'Jesus Christ heals you. **Get up** and roll up your mat.' Immediately Aeneas got up."*
*-Acts 9:34, emphasis added*

*"Peter sent them all out of the room; then he got down on his knees and prayed. Turning toward the dead woman, he said, 'Tabitha, **get up**.' She opened her eyes, and seeing Peter she sat up."*
*-Acts 9:40, emphasis added*

*"Suddenly an angel of the Lord appeared and a light shone in the cell. He struck Peter on the side and woke him up. 'Quick, **get up**!' he said, and the chains fell off Peter's wrists."*
*-Acts 12:7, emphasis added*

During our Revival 101 class, my friend Christina shared a dream she heard about from a friend. In the dream, the Lord said to the dreamer,

I am coming back, and it's sooner than you think.

Sisters, I say to you, it's time to get up! Jesus is coming, and we must be ready for His arrival!

We don't know how much time we have left, and if it's sooner than we think, it begs me to ask: Are you ready for Christ's return? We can get so sidetracked in our situations, bondages, plans, expenses, routines, pain, and even euphoria that there's a possibility we could be sitting down when it's time to stand on our feet. The Lord is longing for his wide-awake Bride to arise!

Some of the meanings of "get up" in the original language are:
to arouse, cause to rise;
to arouse from sleep, to awake;
to arouse from the sleep of death, to recall the dead to life;
to cause to rise from a seat or bed, etc.;
to raise up.

I believe Jesus is standing before us, calling sons and daughters to get up and arise! We have been spectators for far too long. Many have prayed for revival, and now we get to combine our prayers with bold evangelism to see this last end-time harvest brought in! We must get up and go! We must get our households and our bodies in order so that we can pivot with the Lord at a moment's notice.

To those who sit in fear because of the threat of another pandemic or the residual impact of the last one, it's time to **get up** and stand in faith with the perfect love of the Father that casts out all fear. We are to be the most fearless people on the planet because we know who has the final word over our lives! It's not a season of self-preservation but a time to embrace what God has prepared for those who love Him and have been called by Him to bring Heaven to Earth.

*"Only let us live up to what we have already attained."*
*-Philippians 3:16*

To those who have been battling sickness and disease, it's time to **get up** in your spirit and worship Him—the one worthy of worship even in your pain. He may be asking you to take a step of faith and walk out your healing, one step at a time. I do know that regardless of what we face, He is always worthy of our praise and adoration. He has the final word over sickness and the grave!

*"Only let us live up to what we have already attained."*
*-Philippians 3:16*

To those who are sitting at the graveside of loved ones, lost dreams, and aborted vision, it's time to declare to ourselves, "Get up!" We are not bound by the cords of death because we have been given the deliverance of a Savior who paid His life for us to experience resurrection life! Death has been broken and defeated in the life of the believer. So, it's time to speak life to things that have died in your heart so they can experience the resurrection life of Christ. Even with loved ones who have gone on to be with Jesus, I fully believe you can fulfill what they were not able to on this side of Heaven. Ask the Lord to hand those callings to you as your inheritance. There are legacies that were meant to be done and still need to be fulfilled!

*"Only let us live up to what we have already attained."*
*-Philippians 3:16*

To those of you sitting in captivity, the Lord says to you to **get up!** He has declared freedom over you! Your prison of pain is not your palace or refuge! It's time to follow Him out of that prison cell to your personal victory. This was never His intended destination for you. Nor will it be the place you reside any longer. If He is the promise keeper that He says He is, and He sets the captive free, this is your hour of breaking loose. At the name of Jesus, every chain must fall off.

*"Only let us live up to what we have already attained."*
*-Philippians 3:16*

This exhortation is not a word of works but rather a word of invitation to walk in what Christ has already provided for you. We live in the spiritual reality of our inheritance in Christ Jesus. That's the grace of the matter. But may this call to **get up** soar in your spirit with hope that Jesus is not done, and death and sickness and hopelessness and fear do not have the final word over your life. Your citizenship is in Heaven, and Christ is your life! His work on the cross is finished; you aren't going to add anything to it by works. But what changes when we live out of Christ in us, the hope of glory, is the freedom to allow Christ to be manifest in us. He lives His glorious life out of our worship and surrender. He gets to make all things new in us, and the broken places become a highway of holiness upon which we walk. It's not complicated but it does take our permission and surrender. He is good and wants to lavish His abundant goodness on us today in all of these things. It's who He is and what He does!

I bless you in the name of Jesus to **get up** and go wherever He sends you! Don't let counting the cost hold you back; be ready to receive more than your heart could imagine or dream of. It's the hour the Bride of Christ is arising in victory, awakening in fresh power! That's you!

Listen to this worship song: "Stand in Faith" by Danny Gokey

## TESTIMONY

### Raise Your Arms of Praise

A patient was having trouble getting her hearing aid in her ear because her left shoulder was frozen and in pain from two failed surgeries. She explained that the doctor said there was something like a shard in it and surgeries wouldn't work—she would be like that forever. I told her cheerfully that Jesus heals, but she scoffed at my words. She reluctantly agreed to let me pray for her. I prayed a short simple prayer of healing in Jesus' name and asked her to try to lift her left hand. She looked at me like I was crazy and said, "No, I can't lift it. I told you what the doctor said!" I prayed two more times, asking her to check after each prayer. She was aggravated at me, but I gave her my cell number and asked her to text me when Jesus healed it. Within 12 hours, I received a picture of her holding both hands in the air, praising God!

Heather

# Little Girl, Arise

*"The leader of the local synagogue, whose name was Jairus, came and fell down before him, pleading with him to heal his little daughter. 'She is at the point of death,' he said in desperation. 'Please come and place your hands on her and make her live.' Jesus went with him, and the crowd thronged behind. ...*

*"While he was still talking to her, messengers arrived from Jairus's home with the news that it was too late—his daughter was dead and there was no point in Jesus' coming now. But Jesus ignored their comments and said to Jairus,* ***'Don't be afraid. Just trust me.'***

*"Then Jesus halted the crowd and wouldn't let anyone go on with him to Jairus's home except Peter and James and John. When they arrived, Jesus saw that all was in great confusion, with unrestrained weeping and wailing. He went inside and spoke to the people.*

*"'Why all this weeping and commotion?' he asked. 'The child isn't dead; she is only asleep!' They laughed at him in bitter derision, but he told them all to leave, and taking the little girl's father and mother and his three disciples, he went into the room where she was lying.*

***"Taking her by the hand he said to her, 'Get up, little girl!'*** *(She was twelve years old.) And she jumped up and walked around! Her*

*parents couldn't get over it. Jesus instructed them very earnestly not to tell what had happened and told them to give her something to eat."*
*-Mark 5:22-24, 35-43, TLB, emphasis added*

Deep in grief, this father cried out for the life of his daughter. He came to Jesus in desperation and pain. There must have been a mustard seed of hope that Jairus, the synagogue leader, had in Jesus. Religion and law-keeping were pushed aside. This moment called for a miracle, and the only One to do that would be Jesus. Meanwhile, the little girl took her last breath. As Jairus fell on his knees, Jesus' feet began to walk to the little girl. Along came the crowds, the disciples, the ridiculers, the mockers, and the two desperate parents.

Two things were required of Jairus as he walked with Jesus toward the miracle:

1. *"'Don't be afraid (Mark 5:36, TLB).'"* In the face of grief and impossibility, Jesus asked Jairus to leave fear at the door. There's no place for fear when we expect God to do the impossible. Faith and fear cannot coexist. Faith and the fear of disappointment cannot coexist.
2. *"'Just trust me (Mark 5:36, TLB).'"* Believe in the One who is with you. Believe in what He can do with just a mustard seed of your faith. Believe in His goodness and faithfulness. Leave fear at the door and pick up your faith.

Jesus got to the home where mourners were gathered. It's believed that in those days, they hired professional mourners, some of whom decided to take on a mocking spirit and began to ridicule Jesus. He left them behind, protecting the faith of Jairus. Taking Peter, James, John, the mother, and Jairus, Jesus closed the door behind them. It was a sacred space for just a few who were invited into a holy moment of great victory.

The very presence of Jesus brought hope into the room and into the hearts of those five gathered, waiting for a miracle.

*"... in the presence of the God in whom he believed, who gives life to the dead and calls into existence the things that do not exist."*
*-Romans 4:17b, ESV*

Here lay a lifeless little one whom the enemy thought he could snuff out. I wonder what spiritual battle raged over this little one. I wonder if the enemy thought he could silence her because she would be one who would do mighty exploits for Jesus. She was going to have a testimony that would cause many to come to Jesus; and in the enemy's short-sightedness and lack of omniscience, he temporarily muzzled her.

Like the centurion's son, Jesus could have just said a word miles before he arrived at her home.

Like Lazarus, He could have called her out of her room so all the crowds could see and be amazed. And with a word, she would have come back to life.

Instead, Jesus wanted to be near her. He wanted to take her by the hand and let the peace of His presence and the joy of who He is cause her to arise.

He took her by the hand and declared, *"'Talitha koum,' which means, 'Little girl, I say to you, arise (Mark 5:41, NABRE)!'"*

And this is the moment when God looks at each one of us, stretches forth His hand, and places these two words on our spirits: *Talitha koum.*

On your bed of disillusionment, He places His hand in yours and says, "Little girl, arise!"

On your bed of defeat and the end of what seems like dreams hoped for, He places His hand in yours and says, "Little girl, arise!"

On your bed of sickness, He places His hand in yours and says, "Little girl, arise!"

On your bed of waiting and longing and tears, He places His hand in yours and says, "Little girl, arise!"

On your bed of hope deferred, He places His hand in yours and says, "Little girl, arise!"

On your bed of endless storms, He places His hand in yours and says, "Little girl, arise!" (You will walk on water like Peter from this place!)

On your marriage bed of a broken covenant, He places His hand in yours and says, "Little girl, arise!"

On your bed of fear and lack of faith, He places His hand in yours and says, "Little girl, arise!"

On your bed of suffering as your tears water the Earth, He places His hand in yours and says, "Little girl, arise!"

Beloved, this is your moment to take the hand of Jesus and let Him call you forth from death to life, so that dry bones will live again. He has resurrection life to renew in us. This is not the end; this is the beginning of a new chapter, a new day, and a new beginning. He does all things well, and His timing is perfect.

Leave fear and the mocking voices at the door. Close the door and come away with Jesus.

It's time for faith and trust to emerge in you. I pray that these very things will rise up in you.

> Father, thank You for our beds of trial and suffering. James tells us to rejoice in our suffering. So, we lift our hands in worship and thank You that You are not finished with us yet. Let the naysayers and the voices of opposition to our faith be silenced in Jesus' name. I pray for a supernatural deposit of faith to silence fear and to enable us to walk in believing You are who You say You are and that You will do what You promised You will do. I ask for a wall of fire around these ones who need both protection and deliverance. Let this space of protection cocoon them and be a place of healing and resurrection. I pray that You would accelerate their healing and deliverance and supply them with faith as they wait. Jesus, manifest Your goodness, power, faithfulness, and love to them today. Would You allow them to see Your eyes of compassion and to hear

Your words to them, *Talitha koum*? In the merciful and gracious name of Jesus, amen!

Listen to this worship song: "Jesus" by Influence Music

Close with this worship song; let it be your declaration: "Come Alive" by The Belonging Co

# TESTIMONY
## Resurrection Power

Many years ago, my husband and I moved to Raymondville, Texas, to help friends start a church. During this time, we came to know David Hogan and many of his missionaries as their ministry base camp was located in the same town. David ministers in Latin America and has witnessed more than 500 people raised from the dead.

While I was pregnant with my fourth child, we moved to Baton Rouge, Louisiana. I planned a home birth and when I went into labor, I called the midwife. The labor was long and hard, lasting throughout the night. At one point, I felt the presence of the Holy Spirit come into my bedroom and cover me completely. I knew everything would be all right.

Early in the morning, my daughter was born. With the birth of my other children, the midwife would catch the baby and immediately pass her to me to hold and nurse. This time, she grabbed the baby and ran to the bathroom and slammed the door. I saw from the corner of my eye that the baby was blue and not breathing. Later the midwife brought her out and all was well.

Three months later, our family was attending church in Baton Rouge. As I walked into the building, David Hogan was standing at the door. He looked at me and asked, "Where were you three months ago? I was in the Amazon jungle and your face came up before me, and I prayed for you!" His intercessory prayers sent the resurrection power of Jesus into my bedroom the night I was giving birth!

Never underestimate the office of an intercessor. Obedience to pray could mean the difference between life and death!

Suzy

# Walking in Resurrection Power

*"She went and told those who had been with him and who were **mourning and weeping**. When they heard that Jesus was alive and that she had seen him, **they did not believe it**." -Mark 16:10–11, emphasis added*

*"Then Jesus appeared before the eleven apostles as they were eating a meal. He corrected them for having such hard, **unbelieving hearts** because **they did not believe** those who saw him after his resurrection." -Mark 16:14, TPT, emphasis added*

*"So the women hurried away from the tomb, **afraid yet filled with joy**, and ran to tell his disciples. Suddenly Jesus met them. 'Greetings,' he said. They came to him, **clasped his feet and worshiped him**. Then Jesus said to them, 'Do not be afraid. Go and tell my brothers to go to Galilee; there they will see me.'" -Matthew 28:8–10, emphasis added*

*"Then the eleven disciples went to Galilee, to the mountain where Jesus had told them to go. When they saw him, **they worshiped him; but some doubted**." -Matthew 28:16–17, emphasis added*

*"As they **talked and discussed** these things with each other, Jesus himself came up and walked along with them ... ." -Luke 24:15, emphasis added*

*"While they were still talking about this, Jesus himself stood among them and said to them, 'Peace be with you.' They were **startled and***

> ***frightened****, thinking they saw a ghost. He said to them, 'Why are you* ***troubled, and why do doubts rise in your minds****? Look at my hands and my feet. It is I myself! Touch me and see; a ghost does not have flesh and bones, as you see I have.' When he had said this, he showed them his hands and feet. And while they* ***still did not believe*** *it because of* ***joy and amazement****, he asked them, 'Do you have anything here to eat?'" -Luke 24:36–41, emphasis added*

By the looks of it, everyone was a mess! Emotions were running rampant: Some were weeping, some were doubting, some were downcast, some were bewildered, others were amazed. All of a sudden, these Christ followers had their worlds turned upside down. Their Jesus—whom they had loved, followed, and learned from—was gone.

Now what? The disciples were hiding because they feared the Romans, and what they had known with great comfort and safety seemed so fragile at the moment. But the same love that raised Him from that grave kept Him coming back to them to reveal new levels of love. He met Mary Magdalene in her weeping, Thomas in his doubt, and Peter in his need for reinstatement—all because of love. To go from understanding to full, heartfelt comprehension, these disciples needed a fresh experience of Jesus' love.

Jesus never condemned them for their doubt or disillusionment. Instead, He went out of His way to meet them at their place of need. Then Jesus made the greatest deposit of security in His disciples when He came to live within them and set their hearts ablaze. Jesus was so loving and patient in helping His disciples understand the fulfillment of Scriptures about who He is and what His Kingdom is about.

But He also needed them to have a bone-deep revelation about His power and goodness. This was going to be the reality by which they lived. So, He appeared in their gatherings and met them during their fear and weeping. He breathed on them the Holy Spirit (John 20:22) and commissioned them to take the gospel to the ends of the Earth. Their understanding was beginning to increase from an idea in their minds to a passion in their hearts.

As I was sitting with Jesus, I penned these words:

> I am breathing My resurrection life into My Bride today, and she will awaken and go forth! This will not be conceptual but her truest reality. I don't want My Bride stuck. This is not who she is. Just like the men on the road to Emmaus, I will open her heart to really grasp My resurrection power that lives in her. It will change everything for her!
>
> Get ready to walk in new levels of My resurrection power! You are entering a time where everything will look different from here on out. Mark this day and this year because My glory and power are coming like a flood!

We have learned the Scriptures and have a concept of Father, Jesus, and Holy Spirit. Our minds are full of knowledge, but many of our hearts await an encounter with the power of Jesus. It's time for us to live out what we have known, studied, read, and believed! Our hearts are awakening in a new way, just like Jesus experienced in the Garden when the resurrection power of God engulfed Him. It's time to awaken to a love whose surface we have only begun to scratch! This love is not about legalistic obedience and fabricated passion; it's simply about risking our lives on God's character and promises and watching Him bring forth the harvest from such faith.

Jesus knew exactly what His disciples needed when their worlds were turned upside down. He came to them with compassion and truth!

> "In the Gospels we see Jesus weeping over Jerusalem at her upcoming destruction; feeling deep compassion for the large numbers of people who were harassed, distressed, dejected, and helpless; and being moved with pity and sympathy by a leper (see Luke 19:41; Matthew 9:36; Mark

> 1:40–41). Jesus was in touch with a life lived from His heart. Prostitutes and sinners felt at home with Jesus because He was able to sympathize with their brokenness, treat them with deep love and fervent compassion, and enter their world." -Rusty Rustenbach, "Listening and Inner-Healing Prayer"[8]

In the same way, there is a world awaiting our understanding of scripture in such a way that we are compelled with deep love and compassion to run to those who need Jesus. Oh, that this would be the focus of our lives—the increase of His Kingdom here on Earth. Just like Paul stated:

> *"For I am not ashamed of the gospel, because it is the power of God that brings salvation to everyone who believes: first to the Jew, then to the Gentile. For in the gospel the righteousness from God is revealed—a righteousness that is by faith from first to last, just as it is written: 'The righteous will live by faith.'" -Romans 1:16-17*

That was their time; this is our time! We've got the same uncertainties. We've got persecution of the saints brewing now on a global scale and at an epic rate. We all understand fear, sadness, disappointment, and doubt. But that's not the end of the story or a (figurative) place devoid of God. In fact, it's in those places Jesus does His most glorious work and sets your feet to dance! Expect Him to show up in proverbial tombs and to come through walls where we think He will never emerge. Expect Jesus to bring you fish on the shores of your recommissioning. Expect Him to do something so grand that all of Heaven stops to observe when love comes crashing in. This is **who** He is, and this is **what** He does!

> Lord, I pray for those who need You to show up in the places that feel so devoid of Your goodness. I pray that You come crashing in and awaken us to Your resurrection

power in a fresh and new way. Will You do something in our hearts that we have never experienced before? Will You open our ears to a truth our minds, hearts, and souls have never grasped before? Will You pull us close and teach us Your ways that are so much higher than our ways so that they will revolutionize everything for us? I pray that we would indeed awaken to the power that resides inside of us because that is where You live. I pray that You would take us even deeper into Your extravagant love for us, when life just seems messy, and we get flipped upside down. Sort it out and order it for us, Jesus. Place Your peace on it, and then accelerate us into Your timeline and Your purposes. Let those who read these words come alive with greater insight and understanding as to the depth, height, width, and breadth of how Christ loves His Bride! In the mighty name of Jesus, amen!

Listen to this worship song: "Extravagant" by Steffany Gretzinger and Amanda Cook

# TESTIMONY
## Encountering God

In 2012, when I was in the sixth grade, my body developed an intolerance toward gluten. I began having stomach aches when I ate a sandwich or a cookie. My mom suggested I change my diet by cutting out breads, sweet treats, and many snacks that contained gluten. Back then, gluten-free products were just beginning to rise in grocery stores, so I didn't have many options. My lunches consisted of gluten-free peanut butter and jelly made on the driest bread imaginable.

As I moved to the seventh grade, my gluten allergy intensified. I had severe stomach pain if I consumed any trace of gluten. I would cry out to God to take the pain away because it was overpowering. I became nervous over food and food choices, checking ingredients multiple times to make sure gluten was not included. I developed a fear of food that once brought me joy.

One evening, my mom invited me to a healing service that was taking place at a church. After worship, the pastor spoke on healing. A couple of people shared healing testimonies. I clearly remember this moment in worship when the pastor interrupted the song and said, "If you want to be healed, stand up." I felt a pit in my stomach because I knew the Holy Spirit was telling me to stand, even though no one around me did. I wrestled in my seat for 30 seconds before finding the courage to stand. I closed my eyes so I wouldn't notice anyone around me and prayed, "God, will you please heal me of my allergy." At that exact moment, I knew I was healed. I didn't feel different physically, but in my spirit, I knew I had encountered God.

I left the service trying to downplay what had happened, telling myself there was no way God had healed me. When I got home, I wanted to try regular bread but was afraid of a flare-up. Two weeks later, I took a small bite of wheat bread. Five minutes later, I didn't feel anything. Fifteen minutes later, no pain. One hour later, my stomach was normal. I was in shock. God healed me! He healed me from my gluten allergy, and I haven't had stomach pain since.

AnnMarie

# Simply Everything

*"Jesus sat down opposite the place where the offerings were put and watched the crowd putting their money into the temple treasury. Many rich people threw in large amounts. But a poor widow came and put in two very small copper coins, worth only a few cents.*

*"Calling his disciples to him, Jesus said, 'Truly I tell you, this poor widow has put more into the treasury than all the others. They all gave out of their wealth; but she, out of her poverty, put in* ***everything—all she had to live on****.'"*
*-Mark 12:41-44, emphasis added*

Picture a delicate woman in her late 30s. With her head wrapped, she walked into the temple in her tattered dress, perhaps barefoot, with the dirt under her nails from yesterday's work. Too young to have her children support her, she was most likely on her own and alone that day. I wonder where her father and brothers were who would naturally care for her as a widow. Perhaps she didn't own property by which to support herself, so her very meager income had to sustain her. Alone and without a husband, she went weekly to the temple awaiting her Messiah who promised to save her. And sitting nearby, He was there, enraptured by her very person. Jesus watched her every move as she caught His eye. The temple was bustling with all sorts of people from all demographics, but this one woman made Jesus take note.

Her very life became a testimony as Jesus directed the disciples' attention to this one woman. He taught them that following Him would cost them everything. But the sacrifice of worship, when we give all we have, is the defining moment of life truly laid down, as is the testimony of this precious widow.

When you only have two copper pennies, where do you take them?

When you have nothing left, what do you give?

Her response was to give **everything**.

How does a widow who has lost everything give everything? What motivates her toward such deep surrender?

*"'For your Maker is your husband— the Lord Almighty is his name—the Holy One of Israel is your Redeemer; he is called the God of all the earth.'"*
*-Isaiah 54:5*

This widow knew the depth of abandonment to the One she ultimately longed for. Something convinced her that the safest thing was to give everything when she had nothing. Perhaps she remembered the story of Elisha and the widow in 2 Kings—how the Lord supernaturally provided all she needed. In this place of desperation, she gave all her wealth (not just half of it) combined with all of her faith and presented her offering before the Lord. And a testimony of remembrance of her is written in the scrolls of Heaven.

**There are a few others who were willing to give everything.**

*"But the king replied to Araunah, 'No, I insist on paying you for it. I will not sacrifice to the Lord my God burnt offerings that cost me nothing.' So David bought the threshing floor and the oxen and paid fifty shekels of silver for them."*
*-2 Samuel 24:24*

*"When they reached the place God had told him about, Abraham built an altar there and arranged the wood on it. He bound his son Isaac and laid him on the altar, on top of the wood."*
*-Genesis 22:9*

*"While he was in Bethany, reclining at the table in the home of Simon the Leper, a woman came with an alabaster jar of very expensive perfume, made of pure nard. She broke the jar and poured the perfume on his head."*
*-Mark 14:3*

*"He who did not spare his own Son, but gave him up for us all—how will he not also, along with him, graciously give us all things?"*
*-Romans 8:32*

*"You do not delight in sacrifice, or I would bring it; you do not take pleasure in burnt offerings. My sacrifice, O God, is a broken spirit; a broken and contrite heart you, God, will not despise."*
*-Psalm 51:16-17*

Our hearts have to ask these questions, prompted by the faith of the poor widow:

1. If I lost everything in this earthly realm that held me together culturally, economically, and relationally, would I still give Him everything?
2. What compels us to the threshold of such outrageous trust and abandonment?
3. When we have less, do we become more generous toward God because we realize our sustenance comes only from Him?
4. How do we get to a place of such reckless faith that we withhold nothing and waste everything on Him?

The answers to these questions will only be supernatural because they defy the logic of human reasoning. This is the work of Christ in us, the hope of glory!

The gospel message compels us to the point of salvation where we trust Jesus with our very eternity. We declare to Him that we indeed cannot live without Him. We sing to Him that He's the very breath in our lungs, and we know our existence is determined by Him. We trust Him with our future, and we hold onto Him in our suffering. We praise Him on the mountaintops of life. But what do we do with the treasures we hold in our hands? What do we determine is ours, and what is God's?

> "Abandonment is a matter of the greatest importance if you are to make progress in knowing your Lord. Abandonment is, in fact, *the key* to the *inner court*—the key to the fathomless depths. Abandonment is the key to the inward spiritual life." -Jeanne Guyon, "Experiencing the Depths of Jesus Christ"[9]

What is the "everything" that you hold in your hands? If you are indeed *"wretched, pitiful, poor, blind and naked (Revelation 3:17)"* and Jesus owns it all anyway, what is He asking you to place in the offering before Him? Is it your widowhood, your sobriety, your barrenness, your wealth, your poverty, your broken marriage, your prodigal son, your joblessness, or your successes?

The widow is a picture of us in all our need and dependency if we will get to the place of such abandonment and trust. How it captures the heart of Jesus! Again, it begs the question: How do we get to a place of such reckless faith that we withhold nothing and waste everything on Him?

In America, we have chased the great American dream and secured for ourselves barns and bigger barns full of treasures. We have golf tee times and lavish vacations that we love. There's nothing wrong with those. But do we secure our hearts in our earthly treasures and fail to live in the utter desperation of longing for Jesus alone? Is He truly enough and worth the cost of giving our everything? I know that He is, and He is committed to getting us to a place where we believe it as well. If He's the God of abundance, we can trust Him that when we bring Him our **everything** and withhold **nothing**, He will bring the increase. He will indeed bring the provision out of His character, His grace, and His lavish love. But the very thing that must shift is our pursuit of earthly treasures for heavenly ones. Therefore, stake your flag in the ground and declare, "For me to truly live is Christ."

And then, may this prophetic word be said of us in this day:

> "I am about to display a great wave of My authority and My great power and I am looking for a people whose hearts are completely Mine. I am looking for those who are completely consecrated unto Me, for they shall partner with Me to display great moves of My power and presence in this era. They shall be humble, not looking for their own glory and renown but Mine alone. They are My consecrated ones. They shall perform My exploits so that the world may know that I AM. All My children are invited to walk with Me in this way. Many are called, but only those who consecrate themselves will be chosen for what I am about to do in the earth." -Patricia King, "A Prophetic Manifesto for the New Era"[10]

He is worth our **everything**.

Listen to this worship song: "I'm Desperate for You" by Red Rocks Worship

# TESTIMONY

## Triumph of Faith: A Miraculous Healing

I have encountered countless patients in my medical office, but one man's story left an indelible mark on my soul. Tom (disguised patient name) walked into my office burdened with a diagnosis of metastatic prostate cancer. He had navigated hospitals, specialists, and surgeons seeking a glimmer of hope, yet each treatment left him with the same diagnosis.

As I listened to Tom's narrative, the Holy Spirit stirred me to intercede in prayer for Tom. As I prayed, I implored Heaven to intervene in Tom's battle against cancer, petitioning for his deliverance and trusting the Lord to guide the course of his treatment and transform his life.

After months of Tom battling cancer, I had a prophetic dream where Tom walked into my office, radiating joy, and sharing the remarkable news that he had been declared cancer-free. This dream was a divine revelation that awakened my spirit to the possibility of miracles.

Days later, my dream came to reality. Tom walked into my office, his countenance exuding triumph. He proclaimed his miraculous healing, declaring that his cancer markers were no longer present. The verdict of his medical reports confirmed what his heart had known all along—he was free from the grips of cancer. Tom attributed his healing to the power of the Holy Spirit, a force that had defied medical explanation and transformed his life.

Healing knows no bounds. Even in the face of insurmountable odds, miracles are possible when we surrender to the Holy Spirit.

Dr. Alex

DAY 8

# Preparation for a Life of More

*"Joshua told the people, 'Consecrate yourselves, for tomorrow the Lord will do amazing things among you.'"*
*-Joshua 3:5*

*"'Go, consecrate the people. Tell them, "Consecrate yourselves in preparation for tomorrow; for this is what the Lord, the God of Israel, says: There are devoted things among you, Israel. You cannot stand against your enemies until you remove them."'"*
*-Joshua 7:13*

Before Joshua took the Israelites into the Promised Land, there was a time of preparation. It was a time to break camp, pack up, and get their sights set. It was a time to prepare their hearts for what they were about to encounter. They were getting ready to transition their lives into the fullness of God, and in order to do so, some things needed to be released, and some things needed a reset.

Sisters, I believe we are standing at a precipice of expectation and crossing over into even greater fullness and expression of the life of Christ through His people. This next chapter upon us as the Bride of Christ is going to be unlike any we have seen in our lifetime. I believe we are on the verge of even greater levels of supernatural healings, miracles, signs, and wonders. Spiritually dead people need to see the power of God on display! The enemy has lulled them to sleep and spiritual self-sufficiency. Why would they need to give their lives to a seemingly powerless God?

Unfortunately, many of the churches in America have so suppressed the move of the Spirit in and through their churches that even believers are losing focus and passion. Religion and religious activities have us circling places in the wilderness where God never intended for us to go and pitch our tents.

We are in a significant moment of consecration and preparation! Do you feel like your heart is ready to carry what God wants to release through you in this next chapter?

According to the Key Word Study Bible, "consecration" is, "A verb meaning to be set apart, to be holy, to show oneself holy, to be treated as holy ... to dedicate, to be made holy, to declare holy ... to behave, to act holy, to dedicate oneself. The verb, in the simple stem, declares the act of setting apart, being holy (i.e. withdrawing someone or something from profane or ordinary use)."[11]

Will you allow the Lord to take up more space in your heart and life to reveal anything that needs to be released, in preparation for what is ahead? Perhaps there are desert spaces where He needs to meet you to pour out His fullness and abundance. Perhaps there are spaces of resentment and disappointment with God or with others where He wants to pour His love upon. Perhaps there is small thinking He needs to expand before He can take you further. Maybe there are hurts or idols or distractions He wants to speak to you about.

The God of the impossible wants to expand all you know and believe in order for you to cross over into vision, passion, assignment, abundance, promise, and provision.

> "I am about to display a great wave of My authority and My great power, and I am looking for a people whose hearts are completely Mine. I am looking for those who are completely consecrated unto Me, for they shall partner with Me to display great moves of My power and presence in this era. They shall be humble, not looking for their own glory and renown but Mine alone. They are

> My consecrated ones. They shall perform My exploits so that the world may know that I AM. All My children are invited to walk with Me in this way. Many are called, but only those who consecrate themselves will be chosen for what I am about to do in the earth." -Patricia King, "A Prophetic Manifesto For The New Era"[12]

God wants to consecrate and set you apart for what He is about to do in the Earth. You have been appointed for this hour. He is making us a people prepared to carry His presence and His power!

Listen to this worship song: "Your Nature" by Kari Jobe

# TESTIMONY
## A New Creation in Christ

During my senior year in college, I prayed to receive Christ and I became a new and different person. I went to see my parents over Thanksgiving and told them about my conversion. My father's attitude was, "Let's see how long this lasts." I understood what he was saying because I had been interested in different things, and he needed to see if this was real. My mother, on the other hand, said she wanted what I had. She could see the peace, joy, and unselfishness I had found. I was able to explain the gospel to her as it had been explained to me. Although she had attended church as a child and an adult, she didn't have assurance of her salvation. I shared the simple tract that had been shared with me, and she prayed to ask Jesus to come into her life.

A year later, my mom told me she didn't think it had worked because she didn't feel any different. I told her that we don't trust in our feelings, but we put our faith in God's Word and in His promise that, if we ask Him into our hearts, He will never leave us, and whoever has Him has eternal life. She quoted me the Scripture, *"So also faith by itself, if it does not have works, is dead (James 2:17, ESV),"* and she believed that, as a new creation in Christ, she would and should see new life from having been born again. I shared with her how sin separates us from God. I turned to Galatians 5, which lists the sins of the flesh, and asked if she was willing to let God take these things out of her life. I explained that we cannot change ourselves and asked if she was willing to let God remove her sins and give Him control of her life. She said she would need to think about it.

Later, she said she did want to pray and receive Jesus as her Savior and Lord. She accepted His forgiveness and asked Him to make her into the person He wanted her to be. And the angels and her daughter rejoiced!

Patti

# Your Identity is Established with Christ

*"So what do we do? Keep on sinning so God can keep on forgiving? I should hope not! If we've left the country where sin is sovereign, how can we still live in our old house there? Or* ***didn't you realize we packed up and left there for good?*** *That is what happened in baptism. When we went under the water, we left the old country of sin behind;* ***when we came up out of the water, we entered into the new country of grace—a new life in a new land!***

*"That's what baptism into the life of Jesus means. When we are lowered into the water, it is like the burial of Jesus; when we are raised up out of the water, it is like the resurrection of Jesus. Each of us is raised into a light-filled world by our Father* ***so that we can see where we're going in our new grace-sovereign country.***

*"Could it be any clearer? Our old way of life was nailed to the cross with Christ, a decisive end to that sin-miserable life—****no longer captive to sin's demands!*** *What we believe is this: If we get included in Christ's sin-conquering death, we also get included in his life-saving resurrection. We know that when Jesus was raised from the dead it was a signal of the end of death-as-the-end. Never again will death have the last word. When Jesus died, he took sin down with him, but alive he brings God down to us. From now on, think of it this way:* ***Sin speaks a dead language***

***that means nothing to you; God speaks your mother tongue, and you hang on every word. You are dead to sin and alive to God. That's what Jesus did."*** *-Romans 6:1–11, MSG, emphasis added*

Beloved, friend, saint, daughter, glorious bride—that is who you are! When Jesus looks at you, this is who He sees! He doesn't see a sinner, a slave, an enemy, or an orphan. Some of you see yourselves in the second category of identities, but today, He wants to speak a new word to you.

Daughters of the Most High God, the cross has changed everything about your identity. Your identity is anchored in His death, burial, and resurrection. Where Jesus went, you went too, now raised to a new life and a new identity. There's a glorious freedom in forsaking the old wineskin that was your old identity and stepping into who Jesus says you are now: a saint who is now seated with Him in heavenly places. You are marked and sealed, and you belong to Him. You are a new creation, and the King of Kings calls you God's child, not a sinner or a slave any longer.

Lord, for the women reading this today, would You impart their true identity after Your cross, burial, and resurrection? They are standing in a new place, no longer orphans on the outside. They belong to You, and there are many believing women today who don't grasp the transfer of identity that has taken place. Holy Spirit, deposit this truth deep within them. Undo their old belief about their identity, and impart what You say to them today!

**You have been crucified with Christ. Your identity is established with Christ in His death.**

The sin you could not possibly cover on your own (or earn your way out of) was nailed to the cross with Jesus. He looked at a world of sinners and came not only to pay the price for sin but also to make a way for each of us back to the Father. It's through the death of Jesus that your sin was atoned for, and you went from being a sinner to a saint. During this moment at the cross, the greatest sacrifice was made for you.

When you received Christ and died with Him, you were given the ability to die to sin. Your old life was crucified on the cross. Our Sin Bearer took **all** of our sins to that cross so that we are no longer identified as sinners. This is why Paul opens his letters with the phrase "to the saints." It's not consistent with our new identity to sin anymore because we *"have been born of God (1 John 3:9)"*!

So, take those old graveclothes off! Saint, who has been washed clean, you stand not only forgiven—you stand fully redeemed and clothed in garments of holiness.

**You have been buried with Christ. Your identity is established with Christ in His burial.**

This is the greatest turning point for our identity—the past is gone, and the new has come. Baptism models the significance of this moment for the believer. We go under the water (figurative burial) one way, and we come up (figurative resurrection) another. Let's stop visiting the old graves of our old life. Paul exhorts believers in Romans 6 to consider ourselves dead to sin and alive to Christ.

> "We entered the baptismal tank with a cross and we exited with a crown! Sinning is incongruent with our new nature." -Kris Vallotton, "Supernatural Ways of Royalty"[13]

Jesus took all of our sins—past, present, and future—to the grave with Him. We've been crucified and buried, washed by His blood, and now we are daughters of God! We are no longer identified by our sins, so let's leave the past in the past and turn our eyes, hearts, and feet forward. Will you say to Him, "I'm all in with You, Jesus"?

**You have been raised with Christ. Your identity is established with Christ in His resurrection.**

We have been raised to **new lives**. The old is **gone**—dead and buried. It's simply **gone**. Jesus was raised from the grave to give you this new life, but are you willing to walk in it?

> *"We were therefore buried with him through baptism into death in order that, just as Christ was raised from the dead*

> *through the glory of the Father, we too may live a new life. For if we have been united with him in a death like his, we will certainly also be united with him in a resurrection like his." -Romans 6:4–5*

Sisters, we have been called to live up to a higher standard. We no longer try to earn or modify our behavior to gain Christ's holiness and righteousness. Rather, it's who we are, through and through. We get to live according to what Christ says about us because that is how He sees us. This is our true identity, and everything else pertaining to sin and ungodliness is just a false identity. Can you receive the freedom brought by that truth right now?

> "If we've been taught that after receiving Christ we are still sinners, we will struggle with trying to do the right thing because we have put our faith in our ability to fail instead of His work on the Cross! We can spend the rest of our lives living under the curse of our old name, 'sinner,' or like Israel, we can receive our new name that has the power to alter our very DNA. We are saints, holy believers, and Christians, which means we are 'little Christs'! When the Father looks at us, He sees the image of the Son he loves." -Kris Vallotton, "Supernatural Ways of Royalty"[14]

During a very painful season, I had a dear pastor friend say to me, "You are praying like an orphan." I didn't even know what that meant, but it sent me on a journey to understand my identity as a daughter, seated at a royal table, bearing the very image of Jesus. I think we will forever pursue learning about our true identities and living out of what Jesus believes about us.

How about we commit to doing that, beginning today? Repentance is really about coming into agreement with what God says. Will you repent with me today for not believing what God believes about us? Will you turn with me to pursue our true identities in Christ? He has given us a great inheritance in Himself that would take a lifetime to unwrap. But if we can begin to really grasp this and live out of it, I can't imagine how the Kingdom will flow through our very lives. We live out of what we believe!

Lord, would You release the spirit of adoption over my sisters today, so that they would really understand their belonging to You? You accomplished so much in Your death, burial, and resurrection that changed our identities, DNA, and destinies forever. Lord, open wide the gates of our lives so that we would run into wide open spaces of freedom and truth. This reality about our identity isn't a concept to be dissected but rather something You must establish in us by Your Spirit. Jesus, renew our minds with the truth of Your Word and the life of Your Spirit!

Listen to this worship song: "I Am Your Beloved" by Jonathan and Melissa Helser

# TESTIMONY

## Who Am I?

Ashley wanted to read the Bible with someone, so a mutual friend connected us. We slowly started reading the book of John together. She had many questions about the Bible, but she also had concerns in life that distracted her.

Eight months after meeting her, Ashley confessed that her life was empty. Most of the things she placed her identity in had been taken away, and the things she tried to find fulfillment in weren't fulfilling. She knew she needed God, but she didn't know how He could change everything. She told me she struggled to fully trust God because, like a stock market broker, she didn't want to invest in only one option—the risk was high, and the reward seemed uncertain. Yet, here we were, and I knew the Lord brought Ashley to this place to reveal Himself to her.

I shared John 6, which says Jesus is the bread of life and fully satisfies all who come to Him. Still unsure what it meant to follow Jesus, Ashley read how Jesus calls us to deny ourselves, take up our cross, and follow Him. He asks us to make Him our only portfolio investment. I asked Ashley if she was willing to go all in and give Jesus her entire life. Hesitantly, she responded that she was afraid of making such a risky commitment because she was accustomed to depending on her own strength and merit.

I asked, "Has anything in your life—achievements, reputation, social media, parties, friends, clothes, etc.—ever given you true life?" She replied, "No!" I asked, "So, what have you got to lose by following Jesus?" She paused and answered, "Nothing." I asked if she wanted Jesus to be the Lord of her life, telling her she could tell Him if she did. She said "Yes," and we prayed together as Ashley surrendered her life to the Lord. Afterward, she said, "Thank you for never giving up on me." I went home praising God that He never gave up on Ashley or on me.

Hannah

# Identity and Purpose

*"Paul, a servant of Christ Jesus, called to be an apostle and set apart for the gospel of God—the gospel he promised beforehand through his prophets in the Holy Scriptures regarding his Son, who as to his earthly life was a descendant of David, and who through the Spirit of holiness was appointed the Son of God in power by his resurrection from the dead: Jesus Christ our Lord. Through him we received grace and apostleship to call all the Gentiles to the obedience that comes from faith for his name's sake. And you also are among those Gentiles who are called to belong to Jesus Christ.*

*"To all in Rome who are loved by God and called to be his holy people: Grace and peace to you from God our Father and from the Lord Jesus Christ."*
*-Romans 1:1-7*

The Greek word *doulos* is the word by which Paul described himself as a bondservant of the Lord Jesus. It infers complete and utter devotion, where all rights of his own are subjugated to his Master. Paul belonged to Jesus, and his life was, therefore, not his own. So, what was produced in Paul's life and others in Scripture, like James, who also described themselves as slaves or servants of Jesus, was this fruit of belonging and partnering. Out of the identity of a bondservant came Paul's mission: the gospel of God.

Paul knew his calling was clear—to be an apostle was to be a messenger or a special ambassador. His message was the gospel of Jesus to both the Jew and the Gentile. The gospel gave Paul his life mission, vocation, message, and vision. It was the roadmap to which all things tied together and led toward one destination: the reward of Christ Jesus.

The church in Rome was born out of what took place at Pentecost in Acts 2. Paul had longed to get to them, but before he could, he wrote this letter. They were a Church who were incredibly persecuted. Nero would take Christians and sew them into dead animals' carcasses and let the wild animals devour the carcasses and then devour the Christians. He would post their live bodies in the streets and set them on fire to light the streets of the city. Why did Paul not write a letter on how to survive persecution? Why did he reference God 153 times in the book of Romans? God was the most important word in his entire letter to them!

It was imperative that these young believers knew their identity and purpose in the face of extreme darkness and opposition. It was handed to them to also bring the gospel to Rome, the Roman empire, and the nations outside of that. It was not Paul's duty, and they were just called to support him. The same commission that Paul received upon conversion was what every ambassador of Christ Jesus also received: identity and purpose unto Jesus for the gospel. The message of Jesus is our calling! The gospel is our purpose!

Belonging and partnering with Christ until He returns is the goal of every believer born into the family of God, adopted as His son or daughter, infused with the *dunamis* power of the Spirit, and commissioned to a very dark world.

Hear these words of encouragement the Holy Spirit placed on my heart as I processed this passage of Scripture with the Lord.

> A time is coming when the Bride and Bridegroom will have the same voice. We will be speaking the same language. I will not be informing; I will be confirming My Word. I will not be pulling her along; we will move in a synchronized rhythm together. It's going to be effortless for My people to move in the Spirit. They will pray, and I

will answer! They will ask, and their eyes will immediately see the answer. Miracles will become normative! People will testify of My power that will be on display through every submitted vessel.

Do not grow weary because of self-defeat and lack of confidence. You are where I have placed you, and I have not forsaken the work I am doing in you. I am committed to your full restoration. What will result is total confidence in who I am in you. You can do nothing apart from Me. Keep your heart bonded to Me. Apart from Me, you can do nothing.

*"And consider the example that Jesus, the Anointed One, has set before us. Let his mindset become your motivation. He existed in the form of God, yet he gave no thought to seizing equality with God as his supreme prize. Instead he emptied himself of his outward glory by reducing himself to the form of a lowly servant. He became human! He humbled himself and became vulnerable, choosing to be revealed as a man and was obedient. He was a perfect example, even in his death—a criminal's death by crucifixion!"*
*-Philippians 2:5-8, TPT*

Saints of God, we must know who we belong to. You and I are bond-servants of the Lord Jesus Christ. We are in a permanent place of belonging to our King as royalty on Earth. We need not beg or fret; we are bonded to Jesus for all of eternity. Therefore, our lives are not our own. Our Master's business is our assignment on the Earth. We belong with our other family members in unity so the Earth can see Jesus (John 17). Jesus bought us with the highest price: His very life. In humility, He came to us, and we became prisoners of hope (Zechariah 9:12). When we abandon ourselves unto salvation, we abandon ourselves for this life, too. All rights are given to Him for His perfect pleasure and purposes. We know who is King and who sits on the throne of our lives. There we rest securely, confidently, and safely. We take the way of the cross just like Jesus did so that His resurrection power can flow like living waters through the streets.

*"I have been* ***crucified with Christ*** *and I no longer live, but* ***Christ*** *lives in me. The life I now live in the body, I live by faith in the Son of God, who loved me and gave himself for me."*
*-Galatians 2:20, emphasis added*

Saints of God, we must therefore know what we have been called to. Our identity of being a bondservant underscores what flows out of our belonging: the calling and partnering with Christ Jesus to fulfill the mission of God. Paul could state his life mission in seven succinct words—he was *"set apart for the gospel of God … (Romans 1:1)."*

A bondservant indicates complete and utter devotion to the master for the master's business. Here's where we hit the pause button because here is where the battle lies. The enemy wants our total devotion and our hearts' passions to be for everything. So, we tend to our assignments, vocations, relationships, duties, and obligations with excellence and passion and vigor and strength. Our hearts become full of devoted things, but did Jesus ask us to do all of this?

It all begins when we are just toddlers here in America. We train our children to max out their schedules so that they have ample opportunities in college. We train them to be human doings who are addicted to constant stimulation and busyness and wonder why they grow up and don't have any time or desire for Jesus.

If we are going to fulfill the words that the Lord shared with me, we have to eradicate this love affair with busyness. We must break agreement with the idea that everything except being set apart for the gospel is our purpose. We will move in rhythm with Him because we let Him set the pace and determine the course. We have to cut these chains of bondage with busyness if we are going to get on His agenda. It's the way of the cross. It's the fruit of belonging and partnering that will bring to the world the gospel of God. Not my will or my plans or my passions, but Yours, Lord Jesus. It's the only way forward, saints of God.

For the sake of this hour of great urgency, I want to implore our hearts. Let us commit to Jesus our identity as a bondservant and ambassador. Will you ask Him to reset and realign your life with these two identity statements, bondservant and ambassador, **so that** your life can be what Paul's life was—set apart for the gospel of God? If you ask Him, He will faithfully do it. I promise.

To God be the glory!

> Lord, would You anoint our minds and our spirits to receive a transformative word of our identity and purpose just like Paul did? He knew without hesitation to whom he belonged and what he was called to. May it be no different for each of us in this hour.

Listen to this worship song: "Same God" by Elevation Worship

# TESTIMONY

## From Atheist to Evangelist

When I was in Vienna, Austria, I started talking to a man who said he was an atheist. In conversation, the Holy Spirit revealed that this man had a slipped disk in his back. When I asked him about it, he responded, "Yes, I do. How do you know?" After telling him how the Holy Spirit revealed it to me, I prayed for him. As I prayed, he said, "Wow, what is happening?" I answered, "You tell me." He said, "I feel a hand moving the disk back into place." He checked his back and was totally healed. There was no more pain. He was shocked. I shared the gospel with this man, and he accepted Christ into his life.

About five minutes later, he invited me to meet his mom. The Holy Spirit gave me the sense that she had pain in her wrist. When I asked, she said the pain was severe and had been with her for 10 years. I asked her son, who had been saved for five minutes, to pray for her. When she checked her wrist, the pain was gone, and she started to cry. Her son and I shared the gospel, and she also received Christ. This was stunning, as the man went from being an atheist to a believer to an evangelist within a few minutes, leading his mom to the Lord.

Wade

## Straight Paths to Mountaintops

*"A voice of one calling: 'In the wilderness prepare the way for the Lord; make straight in the desert a highway for our God. Every valley shall be raised up, every mountain and hill made low; the rough ground shall become level, the rugged places a plain. And the glory of the Lord will be revealed, and all people will see it together. For the mouth of the Lord has spoken.'"*
*-Isaiah 40:3-5*

*"... fulfilling what was written in the book of the prophet Isaiah: 'Listen! You will hear a thunderous voice in the lonely wilderness telling you to wake up and get your heart ready for the coming of the Lord Yahweh. Make straight every twisted thing in your lives. Bring into the light every dark way. Make right every wrong. Remove injustice. Every heart of pride will humbly bow before him. Every deception will be exposed and replaced by the truth to prepare everyone everywhere to see the Life of God!'"*
*-Luke 3:4-6, TPT*

"Any work of God begins with great preparation." -David Guzik, Isaiah 40 commentary[15]

The words "make straight paths" have been occupying my mind and in my spirit. Can you envision John the Baptist, in all his radical surrender, preceded by the radical surrender of Mary and Joseph, declaring the ancient words of Isaiah? He embodied the very words of God as his life leveled the ground for a grand entrance of the extravagant love of God for humanity—precious Jesus. Someone would have to make straight paths across the spiritual landscape of Earth. And several in this opening scene raised their hands!

> "We are never more fully alive than when we are walking in our divine assignment, producing things for His glory." -Bill Johnson

Can you imagine how these people, who had just endured 400 years of silence from God, were desperately needing level paths to an encounter with Jesus? John essentially says with his life, "I will live a radical demonstration of worship and surrender to usher in the very person of Jesus. I will remove obstacles so you can receive Him and experience the extravagant love of God through Jesus. I will not silence my voice, but I will walk on narrow roads of righteousness so that you have an easy onramp into the arms of Jesus. My life will be an invitation to Jesus, not an obstacle." Peace accompanies straight paths. John was a person of peace to his region and his generation. Although that Scripture was fulfilled in John, it is a now word for us who will prepare the ground for the coming of Jesus!

Many months ago, Peggy Ike, a dear friend and part of the East-West family, who has also traveled with me to many fields, invited a team of women to come to Vancouver, Washington. She has lived there for many years, and God has given her a heart for her city. Her invitation and preparations, both in the natural and spiritual, made straight paths for us to bring Jesus to Vancouver. Peggy is quiet and peaceful and exudes love, but that woman stood as a gatekeeper to her city and opened wide the gate so that the King of Glory would come in. I honor her life of radical surrender and fierce boldness. She is our "John the Baptist" in Vancouver.

Kristin Hill, Julie Shaw, Julie Helton, and Keith Brown have been positioned by the Lord in Waco, Texas. They are passionate about Jesus coming to Waco and the Bride of Christ arising in this hour with fire and focus. They are standing at the gates of their city so that Jesus can come. Our four women of peace have invited teams several times, and Jesus will come as they have asked! These are just a few who are raising their hands to prepare the way of the Lord.

Although John was a direct fulfillment of Isaiah's prophecy, his declaration and plea still resound for us right now. It's time to level the ground in our hearts, remove the mountains, and make straight paths so that Jesus, in all of His extravagance, is encountered through our lives!

**Is my life bringing forth straight paths so that the extravagant love of God walks right out of me, displaying His love for the world He died for?**

*"In all your ways, submit to Him, and he will make your paths straight."*
*-Proverbs 3:6*

*"I instruct you in the way of wisdom and lead you along straight paths."*
*-Proverbs 4:11*

*"The righteousness of the blameless makes their paths straight,*
*but the wicked are brought down by their own wickedness."*
*-Proverbs 11:5*

*"You provide a broad path for my feet, so that my ankles do not give way."*
*-Psalm 18:36*

*"... for I have always been mindful of your unfailing love*
*and have lived in reliance on your faithfulness."*
*-Psalm 26:3*

He does all the work, as we can see by these verses, but it requires our surrender and submission to the process. Will you give Him your yes to do whatever He desires to do to make these straight paths in and through your life for His purposes and His glory?

**Broad, straight paths lead to the coming of the Lord to us and through us. It puts His glory on display through our very surrender to Him! And then He invites us to come up higher to the mountaintops!**

*"Now you are ready, my bride, to come with me as we climb the highest peaks together. Come with me through the archway of trust. We will look down from the crest of the glistening mounts and from the summit of our sublime sanctuary, from the lion's den and the leopard's lair.*

*"For you reach into my heart. With one flash of your eyes I am undone by your love, my beloved, my equal, my bride. You leave me breathless—I am overcome by merely a glance from your worshiping eyes, for you have stolen my heart. I am held hostage by your love and by the graces of righteousness shining upon you."*
*-Song of Songs 4:8-9, TPT*

> "I find it mesmerizing that the most effective position for releasing His heart into the earth is where we have ascended the mountain of our intimacy and trust. High above the distractions of this natural world, we are positioned to wage war on the enemy. We ascend the mountain of the Lord to conquer the mountains of the earth. What an incredibly beautiful picture of ease and strength. You were never meant to wage spiritual warfare from the ground; it was always meant to be done from the high place of intimacy with Jesus." -Christy Johnson, "Releasing Prophetic Solutions"[16]

Beloved, He is taking us up higher in this hour. We have to view the events of the world from Heaven's perspective. We have to see what He sees and pray what Jesus is praying. We can be discerning from sitting with Him in higher places (Ephesians 2:6). Our intimacy with Him soars to new heights and deeper depths as He consecrates us unto Himself. It's sacred, and it's eternal. And as you climb the highest peaks with the Lord, He will give you mantles (your authority and calling when God comes on you in glory) for your life. It's time, sisters, to go to the higher places with Him so that you can walk out the rest of your days in confidence, protection, authority, and anointing!

> I bless you today with an understanding and experience of paths being straightened in your heart and life. I bless you to get ready to summit peaks, hand in hand with Jesus. Tell Him you are ready, and then get positioned to go!

Listen to this worship song: "Come Away" by Bryan McCleery

# TESTIMONY
## Burdens are Lifted at Calvary

She was outside sweeping, or doing laundry, or washing dishes. She was doing one of a hundred domestic chores that occupy the days of a villager in the tea country of South Asia. She told me she was busy but could sit for a bit.

With the help of my translator, I shared with her where I was from, a few details about my family, and why I had come all this way. In the course of our conversation, she shared with me that her husband had left her for another woman, and she had no children. Although she lived with her sister, she felt very alone. And although she didn't say, I could tell she was ashamed to be divorced. Her eyes echoed the sadness in her heart, and her face reflected the weariness in her soul.

Now, I had heard about the power of the name of Jesus, but that day I witnessed it! As soon as I mentioned the name of Jesus, the atmosphere changed. I told her Jesus knows her pain. He sees her. He is waiting with a free and beautiful gift of eternal freedom from shame and guilt, a completely free gift of salvation. His love is complete and perfect, and He will never leave her nor forsake her.

Despite my bumbling and stumbling through my gospel presentation, she hung on every word. With tears streaming down her face, she fell into the loving arms of her Savior. Her face completely changed, and I could see the burdens being lifted off her shoulders. We prayed her prayer of salvation together, and I can honestly say that a new creation stood before me. We hugged and cried and laughed and cried and hugged some more. I truly could have stayed all day. Her name is Vanji, and she is my new sister.

Peggy

DAY 12

# Seeds: It's Our New Normal

*"He also said, 'This is what the kingdom of God is like. A man scatters seed on the ground. Night and day, whether he sleeps or gets up, the seed sprouts and grows,* ***though he does not know how****. All by itself the soil produces grain—first the stalk, then the head, then the full kernel in the head. As soon as the grain is ripe, he puts the sickle to it,* ***because the harvest has come****.'"*
*-Mark 4:26-29, emphasis added*

*"Now he who supplies seed to the sower and bread for food will also supply and increase your store of seed and* ***will enlarge the harvest of your righteousness****. You will be enriched in every way so that you can be generous* ***on every occasion****, and through us your generosity will result in thanksgiving to God."*
*-2 Corinthians 9:10-11, emphasis added*

*"'The seed will grow well, the vine will yield its fruit, the ground will produce its crops, and the heavens will drop their dew. I will give all these things* ***as an inheritance*** *to the remnant of this people.'"*
*-Zechariah 8:12, emphasis added*

As I was preparing to write, the Lord gave me the word "seeds." It is a prophetic picture of the process through which we, as followers of Jesus, are going. He takes that which was of Himself, and He plants it deep within us. Upon our surrender of the soil of our very lives, He begins the process of germination and growth. What will this result in? This will result in what Scripture clearly outlines: a glorious harvest in and through your life.

Let me refresh your memory on the growth of seeds from planting to maturity. According to Indoor Gardening Guide, the three stages of seed germination are:

1. Imbibition: The seed intakes water, swells, and extends its first root (radicle).
2. Dormancy: The seed digests the nutrition inside of it and sprouts.
3. Growth: The seed grows exponentially into adulthood.

There are many words of indictment against the church in America. Some are probably accurate. There are others like, "She's asleep," and, "The church needs awakening," that I tend to ponder with sober mindedness. Look at the stage of dormancy needed for a seed's growth. It's in this place of darkness when the seed looks like it will never come to life, where its greatest growth is both hidden and critical. Then it sprouts. The Bride of Christ may or may not be taking a nap—I've stopped making those sweeping judgments. I know that the Spirit of the Living God is moving and breathing life into hidden places we cannot see. Our very intimate Jesus is all about our rescue, redemption, sanctification, and glorification. If Scripture is clear that He is coming back for a glorious Bride, you better believe He is at work in deeply hidden things that we cannot understand with human reasoning or with an earthly perspective.

> "*How* exactly the seed grows is a mystery to the farmer. Though it grows by a process he cannot see nor fully account for, he has faith in the growing process. So it is with the Kingdom of God: we work in partnership with God, yet the real work is left up to Him—we trust in a process we cannot see nor fully account for." -David Guzik, Mark 4 commentary[17]

Look at the "seed" that was supernaturally planted in Mary's womb that she offered to the Lord. What began as just an embryo became the salvation of all of mankind. We partner with God when we give Him our lives to plant the seed of Himself and His Word deep within. This work that He does is invisible to us, but it is fully known to Him, and He has His eye on the entire process of our growth. We trust in a process we cannot adequately see or perceive, but He is at work. He is making us ready to carry His glory and His power and His presence like never before. Would you receive this word of grace today? Trust the process—however slow it seems to you, however painful, however time-consuming—because God is at work in the deepest and most hidden places of your life. His seed (His very word and His very life) is taking deep root, it's gathering up living water, it's soaking up the light of His presence, and it will burst forth in fruitfulness and glory and growth!

What God has planted in you is for the sake of the world He died for. Your life is a generous offering of the goodness and abundance of God. What He supplies to you, He wants to reproduce through you so that others may find life and provision and healing and salvation. Don't doubt for a moment that your Farmer doesn't have His eye and hand on this process of your life. He doesn't plant and tend and water and cultivate for a dead harvest! Oh no, He's going to bring forth something so marvelous in you, you couldn't imagine it if you tried!

> "This is the glory of Jesus' work in us. It was prophetically said of Him, *a bruised reed he will not break, and smoldering flax He will not quench* (Isaiah 42:3). Jesus takes something as small and insignificant as a seed, buries it, and makes it rise into something glorious. Therefore, we should never despise the day of small things (Zechariah 4:10)." -David Guzik, Mark 4 commentary[18]

**A harvest has small beginnings, but when it comes to full measure, it cannot be denied!**

And here is the hope of what is coming! I believe in this hour of restoration and resurrection power for the Bride of Christ, your little shoot is bursting forth! It will be a harvest of righteousness in and through your life. Your roots are deep in Jesus and will be the anchor for you in the coming season. Beloved, the enemy knows his time is short, and he will not back down. We are going to learn to trust (and war) and follow Jesus in ways we have never had to, especially in America. But we are going to see the power of God on display like never before! And people are going to sit in the shade of our branches and find healing under the tree of our lives. We are in a transition of maturity for the final stage of growth!

*"They will be called oaks of righteousness, a planting of the Lord for the display of his splendor."*
*-Isaiah 61:3b*

Please do not despise the days that feel like slow growth, persecution, and even lethargy. I believe what seems like a setback (or where the Lord seems to have been silent) are our days of critical dormancy where growth is happening, and we can't see it, feel it, or perceive it. So, what do we do? We thank Him, we trust Him, and we don't give up!

Please don't give up on your faith. A harvest is coming, and Father, Jesus, and the Holy Spirit are making you ready to be a glorious oak of righteousness in the coming days. Throw off regret and failure, shame and guilt, and fix your heart on Jesus. He promised He would faithfully complete in you what He began, which started as just a little seed.

I want to close with a portion of a prophetic word from Lana Vawser that the Lord placed on her heart to share:

> "Watch these ones, for they are now arising in the earth, they are coming up out of the wilderness leaning upon Me. They have been in a place of breaking and shaking, they have found My heart in a depth and a way that many do not, because they are not willing to walk the narrow

> path, but these ones are arising in the earth now for the greatest comeback of their lives. They are arising in such deep dependence and humility to carry My heart and the new blueprint of My wisdom and My roar will be LOUD upon them with vindication, favour, provision and revelation, but also My roar THROUGH them will bring forth the manifestation of My Glory and power in ways that have never been seen."

Take heart. Your Overcomer has marked and sealed your life, so trust the process. He is faithful!

> "Then if You're not done working / God I'm not done waiting." -Hillsong Worship, "Seasons"

Listen to this worship song: "Seasons" by Hillsong Worship

# TESTIMONY
## The Move of God Through His Truth

On a mission trip to the interior part of a Latin American country, I was invited to a weekend of ministry. I was told the local pastor/shepherd, who had been ministering at the location for several years, came to the villages once a month, and the people would come out to an open field to hear the Word of the Lord. I was taken to an open field that was all dirt, no trees, located in the center of three villages. The women and men of the village knew Christians from the United States were coming. Around 250 individuals arrived and filled a tent that was set up to host the gathering. I was asked to bring a word from the Lord.

The night before, the Lord clearly spoke for me to speak on Romans 2:11, "*For God does not show favoritism.*" Puzzled, I thought, "What? God why would I bring this scripture? This makes no sense to me. These people are the poorest of the poor, have never met a white person, and barely have food to eat. Of all the Scriptures to bring hope, why would You choose this Scripture?"

Obediently, I stood up the following morning to a silent crowd. I opened the Scripture to Romans 2:11 and expounded on it, reaffirming that God does not look at our means, education, income, status, etc., but God responds to faith. After the message was over you could have heard a pin drop for what seemed like an eternity. I looked around and then said, "If anyone would like prayer, please come forward." Oh my, my, my. The floodgate opened. Everyone rushed to the front of the tent. For the next two and a half hours, we prayed for people. People were weeping, and God was moving. The pastor said that in all his years of ministry, he had never had a move of God like this, and he had never seen any of the village people cry.

God is the same, yesterday, today, and forever. He is the God who responds to faith. Oh Lord, let faith arise in our hearts and lives.

Christina

DAY 13

# Made Ready for This Moment

*"He said to them, 'Go into all the world and preach the gospel to all creation. Whoever believes and is baptized will be saved, but whoever does not believe will be condemned. And these signs will accompany those who believe: In my name they will drive out demons; they will speak in new tongues; they will pick up snakes with their hands; and when they drink deadly poison, it will not hurt them at all; they will place their hands on sick people, and they will get well.'*

*"After the Lord Jesus had spoken to them, he was taken up into heaven and he sat at the right hand of God.* ***Then the disciples went out and preached everywhere, and the Lord worked with them and confirmed his word by the signs that accompanied it."*** *-Mark 16:15–20*

Can you imagine if those signs were manifested daily in our lives? I think I often default to a comfort zone of the unreached mountains of the Himalayas where no one has heard the name Jesus. But what does going look like in a pandemic when people are sick, distressed, distraught, and financially ravaged? What does it look like to head into the grocery store and let our lives be a display of Heaven? The Lord, who had just ascended, left his team of disciples with the Holy Spirit and worked with them to put His power on display to a skeptical and desperate world. I love the language of that partnership! They came out of their quarantine (their hiding) and released revival!

> "We shouldn't wait around expecting that God will change us into someone we're not before He uses us. We have a tendency to say, 'God, if You'll anoint me, I'll go.' God says, 'If you'll go, I'll anoint you.' His plan is to use who we already are—the same people He made us in the first place, with the same personalities, giftings and weaknesses. Just be *you*. God wants to work through you and me. We aren't the main act—God is. But He's made us a crucial part of the breaking in of His Kingdom." -Robby Dawkins, "Do What Jesus Did"[19]

Beloved, Jesus didn't die and commission us to **go** so that we would be safe and without trials, comfortable and sidelined. He died so we would be free, bold, victorious, and carry His glory. I think we have settled for and believed in a kind of comfort-gospel that has actually lulled the Bride to sleep. In this hour, we are being awakened to the truest gospel—the power, signs, wonders, miracles, and reality of the cross and resurrection—to express love for the world Jesus died to save.

I wish I could look you in the eyes and say to you with all my heart, "You have been made ready for this moment!" God has made you ready. It's time to awaken to the destiny He has spoken over your life—the plans and purposes He has spoken. It's time to throw off everything that entangles us and run with passion. What if we lost it all for the sake of Jesus? What if the anthem of our lives became, "For me to live is Christ"? What if we dared to say to the Lord, "I hand You this fragile life, and I ask You to exchange my plans and purposes for Yours"? This is our hour of abundance, not wilderness; fruitfulness, not powerlessness! I think Jesus is standing on His tiptoes waiting for us to step into our glorious moment!

There are places and people that have been assigned to you that no one else can touch right now. He has given many of you the gift to heal; go fearlessly and pray for people. He has given some of you the gift to love people through hospitality. I pray for divine instructions to tangibly love and minister to people right now with your unique and creative expression.

Intercessors, move Heaven with your faithful intercession. No one may see it, but I pray that your knees are metaphorically bruised in this hour while you kneel in the gap for so many. Entrepreneurs, I pray for a release of creativity over you right now for new income streams that will carry many people right now and expand the Kingdom of Heaven here on Earth. Hidden businesses that have a Kingdom agenda, I prophesy that it's time to come out of hiding into the limelight. Doctors, nurses, scientists, pharmacists, I pray for an anointing on your mind for solutions and ideas, and new combinations of medicine for healing. In this shift of the Church into the purposes of God, I pray for a release of grace to flow with every new thing the Lord is doing in the Earth right now—glory to glory.

To my sisters who are apostles, prophets, teachers, pastors, and evangelists, I pray for a double portion of anointing to know exactly how to pivot and move to bring the increase of His Kingdom at new depths, heights, and lengths.

To those of you who are sensing a divine reset in your own heart, don't throw it off. Jesus wept over Jerusalem because the Jews had missed Him in their unbelief, and I believe we can miss Him right now. **He has come to awaken us, not with a shoulder-tap, but with the roar of Heaven!** This is our divine interruption to get us ready for the harvest ahead.

These 40 days are just a glimpse of the intimacy He has for you every day with Him. He's wooing His Bride to a dance of passion and intimacy she needs right now as preparation for Her wedding day. I am praying your life will be marked by the opening Scripture for this day in Mark 16:15–20!

Listen to this worship song: "Christ be Magnified" by Cody Carnes

# TESTIMONY

## The Deaf Hear, the Mute Speak, the Spiritually Blind Receive Sight

I volunteered with 45 other believers from around the world to serve for five days in a medical/dental/vision clinic in the poorest area of the northeastern part of Africa. Not holding a medical or dental license, I was assigned to lead the prayer room for patients who desired prayer. The prayer room had 10 volunteers, along with their interpreters, to share the gospel and pray for the patient.

On the first day of the clinic, we could feel a strong spiritual resistance in an area laden with witchcraft and darkness. On the second day, we were visited by numerous individuals who manifested demonic activity. By the third day, we began feeling a spiritual breakthrough where God graciously favored us with the first notable miracle at the clinic. I was brought to a mother who was there with her 8-year-old son who could not hear or speak.

I put my hands on his ears and over his mouth and commanded his tongue to be loosed in Jesus' name. Immediately, his eyes opened wide in surprise, and he heard me say, "Amen." He then repeated my word, "Amen," and we all jumped for joy with tears streaming down our faces. That miracle opened the door to numerous miracles around the clinic: fevers gone, teeth filled in, eyesight restored, cataracts disappeared, individuals able to walk that could not walk, etc.

The testimonies of the miracles quickly spread into the city and into the local churches. The following day, the clinic was visited by Orthodox priests who were curious about the miracles. We treated the men of God to eye care, and then we opened the Scriptures to them regarding how to be born again. I recall seeing their eyes open while in the prayer clinic, as if the spiritual light went on for the first time in their lives. They said, "We have never seen the Scriptures come alive like this." That day, both priests opened their hearts to the Lord.

While in the city on the last day of the trip, I went into a jewelry store. A Muslim lady asked what I was doing in Africa. I told her about the medical clinic and all the miracles God had done. Before I could stop speaking, the Holy Spirit came upon her and she began to have laughter and joy that she could not contain. She said, "I have never had this before, I cannot stop laughing with joy." I told her that it was the grace of the Lord Jesus Christ, and His presence brings joy. That day, she opened her heart to the Lord Jesus Christ.

There are no limits to the Lord's grace and mercy. I said, "Yes," to God's invitation to join Him in His work, and for that I am eternally grateful.

Christina

# DAY 14

# Partnering with Jesus

*"When Jesus had called the Twelve together, he **gave them** power and authority to drive out all demons and to cure diseases, and he **sent them** out to proclaim the kingdom of God and to heal the sick. He told them: 'Take nothing for the journey—no staff, no bag, no bread, no money, no extra shirt. Whatever house you enter, stay there until you leave that town. If people do not welcome you, leave their town and shake the dust off your feet as a testimony against them.' **So they set out and went from village to village, proclaiming the good news and healing people everywhere.**" -Luke 9:1–6, emphasis added*

After Jesus spent a short period of time modeling the Kingdom to His guys, He was ready to send them out on a test run. He put their training wheels on, ready for the day when He wouldn't be with them anymore but would instead dwell in them by the Spirit. As they went, they healed the sick and cast out demons; they were learning to live and proclaim the Kingdom of God. Their gospel was still walking with them, so they didn't yet have the message of the cross and resurrection. But as they walked with Jesus, they had the Word made flesh being interpreted for them. It was such a beautiful combination of the Word being manifest in the Earth. There they went *"proclaiming the good news and healing people everywhere (Luke 9:6)."* What do you think they proclaimed if they didn't have the cross and salvation from sins as their basis? What was their good news? Was it simply the surpassing love of Jesus they had experienced? What was the message they preached?

I did some research into the original language that underlies *"proclaiming the good news,"* and according to the New Testament Greek Lexicon, it means to bring good news or to announce glad tidings. In the Old Testament, it means to announce the joyful tidings of God's kindness or, in particular, of the Messianic blessings. In the New Testament, it's used especially for the glad tidings of the coming Kingdom of God and of the salvation to be obtained in it through Christ and instruction concerning the things that pertain to Christian salvation.

Can you not sense the eager expectation Jesus must have felt in this moment? He knew His disciples were going to be equipped to do exactly what He was doing. Why wait until after the cross to show them? He could tell them and model it to them, but He might as well throw them in the deep end of the pool. And as they stepped out and went from village to village, people were getting healed and were hearing for the first time about this wonderful man named Jesus. It was so simple, but they had to trust Him and step into it!

And now it's our turn! Oh, the profundity of partnering with Jesus! And this is our commission:

*"'Therefore go and make disciples of all nations, baptizing them in the name of the Father and of the Son and of the Holy Spirit, and teaching them to obey everything I have commanded you. And surely I am with you always, to the very end of the age.'"*
*-Matthew 28:19–20*

*"He said to them, 'Go into all the world and preach **the gospel** to all creation. Whoever believes and is baptized will be saved, but whoever does not believe will be condemned. And these signs will accompany those who believe: In my name they will **drive out demons**; they will **speak in new tongues**; they will pick up snakes with their hands; and when they drink deadly poison, it will not hurt them at all; they will **place their hands on sick people**, and they will get well.'" -Mark 16:15–18, emphasis added*

We have the Great Commission (following the resurrection) and the promised Holy Spirit living inside of us. We have the full gospel message and Jesus living in us to demonstrate the gospel. This can be the lifestyle of all believers! Jesus made it possible for us because He promised it, and He never goes back on His word.

But the interesting thing about Luke 9:1–6 is that He sent them out with power before the cross! And they were to take nothing in addition. Now we really don't have any excuses!

> "You don't need the Holy Spirit if you are merely seeking to live a semi-moral life and attend church regularly. You can find people of all sorts in many religions doing that quite nicely without Him. You only need the Holy Spirit's guidance and help if you truly want to follow the Way of Jesus Christ. You only need Him if you desire to 'obey everything' He commanded and to teach others to do the same (Matt. 28:18–20 NIV). You only need the Holy Spirit if you have genuinely repented and believe. And you only need the Holy Spirit if you understand that you are called to share in Christ's suffering and death, as well as His resurrection (Rom. 8:17, 2 Cor. 4:16–18, Phil. 3:10–11)." -Francis Chan, "Forgotten God"[20]

Jesus modeled what it looked like to proclaim good news for them in Luke 8:1–3:

*"After this, Jesus traveled about from one town and village to another, proclaiming the good news of the kingdom of God. The Twelve were with him, and also some women who had been cured of evil spirits and diseases: Mary (called Magdalene) from whom seven demons had come out … and many others."*

Paul modeled this for us:

*"I came to you in weakness with great fear and trembling. My message and my preaching were not with wise and persuasive words, but with a demonstration of the Spirit's power, so that your faith might not rest on human wisdom, but on God's power." -1 Corinthians 2:3–5*

> "But God calls his disciples to embrace both the truth of his Word *and* the power of His Spirit—both are essential ingredients for living the life Jesus made possible. No doubt, we will need to rely on God's wisdom and exercise courage to remain faithful to this critical balance taught and illustrated in Scripture." -Bill Randall, "The Life Jesus Made Possible"[21]

We are coming into a period of time just like when the baby Church was sent out from Jerusalem to the ends of the Earth, and we can't sit back anymore. Jesus has put a roar in us to push back the kingdom of darkness and release the Kingdom of God in the Earth. We are the only ones called, commissioned, and sent out to advance the gospel. And we are the only ones assigned to this time in history. If we are going to see the return of Jesus in our lifetime and speed His return, we must go! We must get out of the spectator seats and into the harvest!

> "There is a cry among God's people. There is a passion being born, a thirsting for the power and glory of God to permeate the earth. ... A certain sense of dissatisfaction has to come in the Body of Christ, a sense of restlessness to want more of His power manifested ... . We should all be an explosive representation of His power on the face of this earth." -James Maloney, The Dancing Hand of God[22]

This is the life Jesus made possible for you, and there are 3.4 billion people who have yet to hear His name. As part of these 40 days of intentionally pursuing Jesus, will you look at His face as He eagerly sends you to take His love and power into the harvest field? The world needs your beautiful feet!

Simply pray these three words and see what He will do: **Jesus, send me.**

Listen to this worship song: "Beautiful Jesus" by Passion

## TESTIMONY
### Serving One Master: Jesus

On a mission trip to South Asia, trekking through the Himalayan foothills to visit unreached villages, we came to a small house at the end of the village. A thin, quiet, and shy young man, Shiva, stood in his front yard and welcomed us to talk with him. We learned that his wife worked in tea gardens, and he stayed home during the day to work on their house and care for his young son, his deaf-mute brother, and his deaf grandmother.

His tattered shirt and pants were sweaty from a full day's work, and I noticed his shoes were too big and stayed on his feet by tying the laces around his ankles, which were bleeding. He had the face of Buddha tattooed on his forearm, and he was wearing a red thread necklace with a large Buddha pendant. He shared his allegiance to following Buddha but couldn't answer with certainty what would happen to him when he died.

As we shared the gospel with him, the good news that he no longer had to work for his salvation but that Jesus paid for his sins and wanted to give him the gift of grace, his entire body posture seemed to relax as if a weight was being lifted from his shoulders. Without hesitation, he said, "Yes, I want to receive Jesus." We prayed with him and, afterward, with a smile on his face and enthusiasm in his voice, he invited us into his home to meet his son, brother, and grandmother. We prayed for each of them.

As we prepared to say goodbye, my translator and I felt the Holy Spirit tell us to communicate to Shiva that he cannot serve two masters and can no longer worship any idols or Buddha. We pointed to the necklace he was wearing. He immediately touched the necklace while we were explaining to him what idols are. We could sense the hesitancy that he had to take off the necklace, and I could see it was probably one of the few things he owned that had any importance. We told him it was fine to wear jewelry, and we tried to help him untie the Buddha pendant from the red thread that he could continue to wear. Suddenly, with two hands, he ripped the necklace off over his head. In that moment, it had such significance that he really understood he could let go and give up all the things that he used to perceive as high value and importance to receive the one that mattered—a relationship with Jesus. We all cried and exchanged big hugs. I'll never forget this young man named Shiva.

Kelly

DAY 15

# The Inclusivity of Christ

*"'Teacher,' said John, 'we saw someone driving out demons in your name and we told him to stop, because he was not one of us.'*

*"'Do not stop him,' Jesus said. 'For no one who does a miracle in my name can in the next moment say anything bad about me, for whoever is not against us is for us. Truly I tell you, anyone who gives you a cup of water in my name because you belong to the Messiah will certainly not lose their reward.'"*
*-Mark 9:38-41*

*"It's true that there are some who preach Christ out of competition and controversy, for they are jealous over the way God has used me. Many others have purer motives—they preach with grace and love filling their hearts, because they know I've been destined for the purpose of defending the revelation of God.*

*"Those who preach Christ with ambition and competition are insincere—they just want to add to the hardships of my imprisonment. Yet in spite of all of this I am overjoyed! For what does it matter as long as Christ is being preached? If they preach him with mixed motives or with genuine love, the message of Christ is still being preached. And I will continue to rejoice .... Whatever happens, keep living your lives based on the reality of the gospel of Christ. Then when I come to see you, or hear good*

*reports of you, I'll know that you stand united in one Spirit and one passion—celebrating together as conquerors in the faith of the gospel."*
*-Philippians 1:15-18, 27, TPT*

"... *For whoever is not against us is for us (Mark 9:40)"* has been resounding in my mind. Perhaps these words of Jesus stand in direct conflict with what we normally hear, "If you're not for me, you're against me." Jesus flips that statement right here. I love His inclusivity and wide-open arms!

In the passage from Mark, either John the Baptist's disciples or some of the 70 who were sent out by Jesus (Luke 10:1-7) were moving with signs and wonders. Demons were being cast out, and it was not from one of the 12 disciples. Tensions were rising. How could other followers of Jesus cast out demons, they asked? Later on in the New Testament, Paul was faced with something somewhat similar, and we see that territorialism, cynicism, or criticism escaped Paul.

**It drills down to one question: Is the gospel being preached?**

Do you know how many denominations there are in the Christian faith? According to Live Science, there are more than 45,000 denominations worldwide. "Followers of Jesus span the globe. But the global body of more than 2 billion Christians is separated into thousands of denominations."

**Again, is the gospel being preached, or are we busy staying divided?**

I find it humorous that the disciples were more frustrated that some other Christ follower could cast out demons, but they couldn't. It wasn't about celebrating the freedom of the demon-possessed person but rather their own territorialism on the demon-possessed. Unfortunately, it's not a new issue for the Bride of Christ. Competition and cornering the market on ministry or theology have kept us all the more divided. Somehow, instead of seeing the vast abundance of the Kingdom of God coming to Earth, we are vying for market share, and popularity, while being concerned with not offending the world.

Let us get back to these truths and view one another with this eternal perspective:

*"I urge you, my brothers and sisters, for the sake of the name of our Lord Jesus Christ, to agree to live in unity with one another and put to rest any division that attempts to tear you apart. Be restored as one united body living in perfect harmony. Form a consistent choreography among yourselves, having a common perspective with shared values."*
*-1 Corinthians 1:10, TPT*

*"And you also were included in Christ when you heard the message of truth, the gospel of your salvation. When you believed, you were marked in him with a seal, the promised Holy Spirit … ."*
*-Ephesians 1:13*

*"… so in Christ we, though many, form one body, and each member belongs to all the others."*
*-Romans 12:5*

*"Accept one another, then, just as Christ accepted you, in order to bring praise to God."*
*-Romans 15:7*

*"So from now on we regard no one from a worldly point of view. Though we once regarded Christ in this way, we do so no longer."*
*-2 Corinthians 5:16*

*"There is neither Jew nor Gentile, neither slave nor free, nor is there male and female, for you are all one in Christ Jesus."*
*-Galatians 3:28*

*"In your relationships with one another, have the same mindset as Christ Jesus … ."*
*-Philippians 2:5*

*"Whatever happens, conduct yourselves in a manner worthy of the gospel of Christ. Then, whether I come and see you or only hear about you in my absence, I will know that you stand firm in the one Spirit, striving together as one for the faith of the gospel .... "*
*-Philippians 1:27, emphasis added*

The enemy wants nothing more than for us to be divided and polarized against one another. If he can defeat the very prayers that Jesus prayed for us in John 17 before bearing the cross, Satan would claim such victory. The Spirit of God will give us unity because it's how Father, Son, and Holy Spirit exist. It's who They are and the essence of Their relationship with one another and with us. So, unity isn't a by-product; it's the very foundation of our relationships. But Jesus also wants us to fight for it. We have to fight to maintain our unity with one another.

Have we lost sight of living for "that day" in order to preserve our lives and maintain our strong stance on any earthly topic? Let's get our gaze and perspective from where we are seated in heavenly places. Can we please be the answer to the cries of Jesus' heart in John 17?

*"My prayer is not for them alone. I pray also for those who will believe in me through their message, that all of them may be one, Father, just as you are in me and I am in you. May they also be in us so that the world may believe that you have sent me. I have given them the glory that you gave me, that they may be one as we are one—I in them and you in me—so that they may be brought to complete unity. Then the world will know that you sent me and have loved them even as you have loved me.*

*"Father, I want those you have given me to be with me where I am, and to see my glory, the glory you have given me because you loved me before the creation of the world.*

*"Righteous Father, though the world does not know you, I know you, and they know that you have sent me. I have made you known to*

*them, and will continue to make you known in order that the love you have for me may be in them and that I myself may be in them.'"*
*-John 17:20-26*

I will leave you with this closing question: Is the gospel being preached through your life? It's got to boil down to that one question in this hour because there are still more than 3.4 billion people waiting for you to tell them about Jesus!

Listen to this worship song: "Nothing/Something" by Pat Barrett and Dante Bowe

# TESTIMONY
## Spiritual, Emotional, and Physical Healing

I was asked to teach an auditorium filled with women on how to share the gospel. It was a full day of teaching with breaks every two hours. Before the lunch break, I invited those who wanted prayer to come forward. Many women walked away with breakthroughs, and one woman received a notable physical miracle. This lady was last in line, sitting in the pew with a cane in her hand. She was diagnosed with fibromyalgia and had not walked without a cane for two years because of the intense pain and weakness in her body.

The Holy Spirit instructed me to ask her some questions about her past, specifically her divorce. I saw in the Spirit a python-looking spirit wrapped around her, suffocating her. The Holy Spirit showed me that abusive words of her ex-husband had bound her and allowed this python-looking spirit to squeeze the life from her. She affirmed that her husband had been emotionally and verbally abusive.

We prayed together, forgiving her ex-husband, and then we renounced his negative words over her. Immediately, she said it felt like lightning going through her body from her head to her feet. She then jumped up and began to run around the aisles of the church, without her cane, praising the Lord for what He had done. The Lord freed her from demonically engineered words that were attached to her life when she forgave her accuser.

The Lord is our wonderful advocate. He knows how to thoroughly plead our case and win. All glory to God—to Him be all glory, honor, and praise.

Christina

# Make Preparations

*"'And you, my son Solomon, acknowledge the God of your father, and serve him with **wholehearted devotion and with a willing mind**, for the Lord searches every heart and understands every desire and every thought. If you seek him, he will be found by you; but if you forsake him, he will reject you forever.'"*
*-1 Chronicles 28:9, emphasis added*

*"May he **strengthen your hearts** so that you will be blameless and holy in the presence of our God and Father when our Lord Jesus comes with all his holy ones."*
*-1 Thessalonians 3:13, emphasis added*

*"Therefore, **with minds that are alert and fully sober**, set your hope on the grace to be brought to you when Jesus Christ is revealed at his coming. As obedient children, do not conform to the evil desires you had when you lived in ignorance. But just as he who called you is holy, so be holy in all you do; for it is written: 'Be holy, because I am holy.'"*
*-1 Peter 1:13-16, emphasis added*

The Spirit placed these words on my heart:

Prepare your heart and mind for action.

I was so intrigued by the charge, and yet I didn't know how to do this, practically speaking. "Lord, what does this even mean when You say this?" I pondered this charge for days.

As the world is rapidly changing, Christendom as we know it is in a profound pivot, and believers are being pummeled by the enemy. There's an acceleration of events taking place on the biblical calendar, and the Bride is awakening. It's time to make preparations for His coming. It's the sort of moment the disciples had in the upper room with Jesus before and after His death. They were preparing for a moment with their Savior that was unexpected. So it is with us, in this historical moment. We must get to the upper room and make preparations as we ready our hearts and minds for a time and a season we have not ever walked through.

> "More than anything, this moment requires those of us in positions of authority (and even most of us who are not) to embrace an *adventure-or-die* mindset, and find the courage and develop the capacity for a new day. We are heading into unchartered territory and are given the charge to lead a mission where the future is nothing like the past." -Tod Bolsinger, "Canoeing the Mountains"[23]

What is being required of those of us daring to go with Jesus is a heart and mind prepared for action. That means the clutter and cobwebs are cleared out! The idols of the heart and the things that hold our minds captive are submitted to the loving counsel and housekeeping of the Holy Spirit. The gardens of our lives need to be intimately tended by the One who prunes the vines. As I dive into these two segments, let's get ready. Time is ticking, and we have a race to finish!

Make this your prayer right now:

*"Test me, Lord, and try me, examine my heart and my mind … ."*
*-Psalm 26:2*

## Circumcise Your Heart

*"The Lord your God will circumcise your hearts and the hearts of your descendants, so that you may love him with all your heart and with all your soul, and live."*
*-Deuteronomy 30:6*

In Hebrew, the word for circumcise is *muwl*, also meaning to cleanse, circumcise, let oneself be circumcised, cut, and be cut off. It's a removal of all the complications, idols, distractions, and clutter so that we can be the ones who belong fully to the Lord. It's a cutting process that we give permission to the Lord to undergo. He does it with a physician's precision and shepherd's care because He knows what is causing us heart disease and an irregular heartbeat. He wants us to be whole and healed and have our heartbeat in rhythm with His own for more than just temporary affairs. It's a matter of belonging and being so intimately known by Him for the sake of simple devotion and a life of great flourishing.

> "I knew Jesus, and He was very precious to my soul; but I found something in me that would not keep sweet and patient and kind. I did what I could to keep it down, but it was there. I besought Jesus to do something for me, and when I gave Him my will, He came to my heart, and took out all that would not be sweet, all that would not be kind, all that would not be patient, and then He shut the door." -George Fox

Pray this prayer with me to clean up our hearts:

> "For myself and my ancestors, I renounce and repent for having a heart that has grown fat with spiritual plaque. I repent for hard heartedness and for allowing my heart to grow dull, my ears to become hard of hearing and my

eyes to become dim and blind. For myself and my family line, I repent for and renounce hardening our hearts to the voice of God. I repent for and renounce saying any words to suggest or declare that God doesn't hear, see or care about our situation." -Paul L. Cox, Brian P. Cox, and Barbara Kain Parker, "Generational Prayers"[24]

Lord, I ask You now to ignite my heart with a fresh passion and desire for intimacy with You. Would You come and cut off anything that has held me back in obedience and consecration? Tend to my heart afresh today. I give you permission to circumcise my heart with Your precision and kindness.

## Renew Your Mind

*"Do not conform to the pattern of this world, but be transformed by the renewing of your mind. Then you will be able to test and approve what God's will is—his good, pleasing and perfect will."*
*-Romans 12:2*

*"... for, 'Who has known the mind of the Lord so as to instruct him?' But we have the mind of Christ."*
*-1 Corinthians 2:16*

In Greek, the word for "mind" means comprising alike the faculties of perceiving and understanding and those of feeling, judging, determining the intellectual faculty, the understanding reason in the narrower sense, as the capacity for spiritual truth, the higher powers of the soul, the faculty of perceiving divine things, of recognizing goodness and of hating evil.

Having the mind of Christ means that we as believers have the ability to share the plans, purposes, and perspectives of Christ. We see things from His vantage point and have His insight and discernment on all matters.

Because He is not shaken, neither are we. We are seated with Him in heavenly places so our ears are tuned to the things He shares with us from the throne room of Heaven. That truth, spoken into our innermost being, should shift the counsel of our hearts and the decisions of our will. It's from this place with Jesus that we ask the Lord to renew our minds so that we think and move and have our being from this place of truth, informed by intimacy with Christ. It's a necessary process of preparation in order to finish this race. Many will fall away in the last days. Let that not be us, Lord Jesus, because we are operating fully with the mind of Christ!

Pray this prayer with me to prepare our minds for action:

> Lord, we repent for allowing our minds to become sidetracked, distracted, and informed by the world. Forgive us for not desiring Your Word or Your counsel and for doing things our way, with human reasoning. We repent for having minds that are tantalized by the world and not the Word of God. We repent for our intellectualism, humanism, and ungodly logic and reasoning. Renew and refresh our minds today so Your plan, purpose, and perspective become ours. Align our thoughts with Your thoughts and ready us for action, so that we would hear the Word of the Lord and move on it. Deliver us from double-mindedness, second-guessing, doubt, fear, and an unsettled mind when it comes to Your Word, Your voice, and Your invitation to follow You.

Beloved of the Lord, it's time we head to the upper room for a while and spend time seeking His heart for the days ahead. Make preparations. He is coming for a Bride who is wide-awake, yet many of us are exhausted over worldly matters and distractions. This hour is calling for the intentionality of intimacy so that we can move in lockstep with the Spirit into the greatest harvest field awaiting you and me.

*"And the peace of God, which transcends all understanding,*
*will guard your hearts and your minds in Christ Jesus."*
*-Philippians 4:7*

Listen to this worship song: "Tend" by Emmy Rose and Bethel Music

## TESTIMONY

### Hope Restored: A Heart Made Whole

While on mission in Latin America, I met a woman who had sadness in her eyes, a spirit of anxiety and oppression over her, and a heavy heart. As we talked, she started to cry and shared how she had awoken that morning with chest pains. She said she couldn't breathe very well, and it felt like someone was sitting on her chest. She had a feeling of hopelessness. As I shared the message of Jesus, her chest started to feel better. I told her that Jesus is a miracle worker and desires to heal and repair the broken parts of our hearts and bodies. I immediately prayed for healing for her heart, both physically and spiritually. I prayed for relief from the anxiety and for smooth breathing for her lungs. After praying, her eyes filled with tears as she said her pain was gone, her breathing was normal, and the anxiety had disappeared. She asked, "How did you do that?" I told her it wasn't me; it was Jesus through me who healed her. She gave her life to Jesus, joyful and thankful that her heaviness of heart and physical pain were gone.

Becky

# It's Hunting Season

*"We have escaped like a bird from the fowler's snare; the snare has been broken, and we have escaped. Our help is in the name of the Lord, the Maker of heaven and earth."*
*-Psalm 124:7-8*

*"Surely he will save you from the fowler's snare and from the deadly pestilence. He will cover you with his feathers, and under his wings you will find refuge; his faithfulness will be your shield and rampart."*
*-Psalm 91:3-4*

To have a successful hunting season, there are several necessary players and objects needed. First, you must have a fowler or a hunter. This fowler must have his weapon and have not only been studying his prey but practicing his shot. The fowler must also have a well-constructed trap to catch unsuspecting prey. Next, you have the innocent bird, simply living life in its environment with its bird buddies. It seeks survival, protection, and refuge like every other bird. The fowler will need the necessary bait to catch the prey in the trap or kill it with a finely fashioned weapon. With all these things in hand, you have the perfect setup to bring home the bounty of your kill.

I took a deep dive into these two Scriptures while I was in Alaska, which is a land teeming with hunters, prey, and traps. As winter rolls in, Alaskans have been busy fishing and hunting, storing their food for the winter. In those cold, dark months, both man and beast seek to survive.

The bears have filled their bellies in preparation for hibernation. The Lord began to speak to me about the sneaky hunter, baiting his unsuspecting prey, and God's refuge and protection over His people.

> "Fowlers have many methods of taking small birds, and Satan has many methods of entrapping souls. Some are decoyed by evil companions, others are enticed by the love of dainties; hunger drives many into the trap, and fright impels numbers to fly into the net." -Charles Spurgeon

Do you know that your enemy studies you? He knows your weaknesses, and although his methods are tried and true, they are not new, nor are they creative. He sets a trap for your feet, baits it according to your cravings and propensities, and then he waits, prowling undercover (1 Peter 5:8). Meanwhile, you fly in to taste just one of the delicacies waiting for you, and the weapon fashioned just for you wounds your soul. The clever enemy of your life works in secret, devising a plan for your destruction. Once you have outwitted him, he will change his trap or even his strategy. Remember, he has studied you. He knows what pleasures you and exactly what he needs to do to arrange for your demise. He's crafty, ferocious, and cunning, waiting quietly in the shadows. Meanwhile, you, the unsuspecting and darling little bird, fly about in vulnerability and often innocence. He laughs as he wounds you. He chuckles as he ties a chain around your ankle so you can't soar like you used to. Bait after bait and trap after trap, and this once free and innocent bird finds itself bound, broken, and wounded.

Sounds like so many of our stories in one hunting season or another, doesn't it? But that's not the end of the story!

> "If Jehovah had not helped, how great would have been the calamity! But He has helped, and the sigh which trembles with the consciousness of past peril, merges into the glad song: Blessed be Jehovah." -G. Campbell Morgan

*"Our help is in the name of the Lord, the Maker of heaven and earth."*
*-Psalm 124:8*

*"He will cover you with his feathers, and under his wings you will find refuge; his faithfulness will be your shield and rampart."*
*-Psalm 91:4*

*"'For the Lord your God is the one who goes with you to fight for you against your enemies to give you victory.'"*
*-Deuteronomy 20:4*

*"'They will fight against you but will not overcome you, for I am with you and will rescue you,' declares the Lord."*
*-Jeremiah 1:19*

*"The Lord is a refuge for the oppressed, a stronghold in times of trouble."*
*-Psalm 9:9*

*"Keep me free from the trap that is set for me, for you are my refuge."*
*-Psalm 31:4*

*"The Lord is my rock, my fortress and my deliverer; my God is my rock, in whom I take refuge, my shield and the horn of my salvation, my stronghold."*
*-Psalm 18:2*

He has given us weapons for warfare. He does not leave us uncovered. He gives the strategy of worship as we exalt our victorious One. He has given us the counsel of the Holy Spirit to warn, shepherd, correct, and guide us. We have our armor (Ephesians 6) to be dressed in for the days of battle. We have the blood of Jesus to cover and cleanse and heal. He has given us His Word by which our minds are renewed and transformed. The power of prayer breaks strongholds and puts thousands to flight. The cross and resurrection sealed our victory over the enemy so that we can walk free of guilt and shame, wounding and regret. He is on our side, and He has not forsaken His people.

We are victors, not victims, in this war over our lives. If Jesus says that about His overcoming ones, that truth must begin to rise in us. We must stand steel-toed before the enemy. We must know who our companions are and the propensity of our broken humanity to fall into one trap after another, often because of whom we associate with. **Do your close companions willingly or unwittingly set traps for your feet or battle with you for your victory?**

*"'Among my people are the wicked who lie in wait like men who snare birds and like those who set traps to catch people.'"*
*-Jeremiah 5:26*

These days require utter and total dependence on Jesus because a tsunami of tactics has been unleashed across the Earth to sideline, destroy, and cripple God's people so we would be bound and ineffective before Jesus returns. That's the truth of these days. But if Jesus has come to heal and set His people free and to fulfill His promises for each one of us, you better believe He will stop at nothing to rescue you from the trap and heal you from the fowler's wound.

> "As the bird could not get out of the snare, so the soul cannot escape from temptation; but God can bring it out, and he works the rescue. Hear this, ye that are slaves to drunkenness: God can deliver you. You that have fallen into licentiousness hear it—God can deliver you. Whatever the sin that has birdlimed you, that gracious hand which once was nailed to the cross can set you free." -Charles Spurgeon

To those emerging from the snare, throw off shame and regret and fall into the arms of Jesus. There's too much ahead to live in the wilderness of past mistakes. Great will be your authority in ministry on the other side of your healing.

To those caught in a trap, it's time to ask your godly companions to pray you to victory, wholeness, and freedom.

To those unsuspecting birds sitting on a branch in your bird refuge with no apparent threat, remember you have an enemy studying you to take you out. These are not days to be unwise about the schemes and strategies of our enemy.

*"Moreover, no one knows when their hour will come: As fish are caught in a cruel net, or birds are taken in a snare, so people are trapped by evil times that fall unexpectedly upon them."*
*-Ecclesiastes 9:12*

*"'Be careful, or your hearts will be weighed down with carousing, drunkenness and the anxieties of life, and that day will close on you suddenly like a trap.'"*
*-Luke 21:34*

I want to close by declaring a powerful prophetic word I read as I was spending time with the Lord in all these passages of Scripture. The timing of its release was profound. Take hold of it and declare it over your life and your loved ones!

> "All demonic negotiations happening in the Spirit realm against you and your family are broken now! Lord release confusion in the encampment of darkness. What tormented you will not follow you into the next season, the Lord is closing the door to your past. Those who have plotted against you will stumble and fall into their own entrapments. What your enemies have planned for your downfall, I decree the Lord will turn it around for a testimony. I pray the Lord would grant to you full access

to Heaven's storehouse. Angelic assistance is set to deliver you from destruction and aid you in your proper position. Everything concerning the affairs of your life is being set in order, the demonic entrapment is finished in the mighty name of Jesus! The wind of change is blowing everything into place, get ready to catch a fresh wind!" -Charlie Shamp

In the mighty name of Jesus, amen!

Listen to this worship song: "See a Victory" and "Surrounded" by Elevation Worship, featuring Brandon Lake

# TESTIMONY

## Guilt and Shame Removed, Cancer Healed

I recently met with a young lady who had overcome three cancers and was in the midst of a second round of chemo for a diagnosis of multiple myeloma. While ministering to her, she could not get over the guilt and shame she felt for what she perceived as having failed in raising her children, blaming herself for their current state. With great sorrow of heart, she repented. After she spoke, I asked if **she really believed** the message of the cross. Then I asked, "What is the message of the cross? Was it not that Jesus Christ, not you and me, took and carried away our sin and shame, along with the debt we owed due to sin?"

Although she fully believed God could save her, the great amount of guilt and shame she was carrying in her heart was keeping her from **giving and receiving** forgiveness from the Lord. On this day, however, the miracle light went on in her heart. She got it. She knew she needed to release and receive. She prayed, transferring her guilt to Christ and receiving His perfect atonement and healing of her body and soul. When she was finished, God released His *dunamis* power, His miracle working power, into her body. We then took communion.

When I arrived at her home, she was bedridden. When I left, she was walking around. Seven days later, I received a text from her. After three rounds of chemo, her positive numbers were off the chart and the negative numbers were excessively low. I also received this note from her: "The Lord spoke to me this morning, the first time in 30 years. I heard and knew His presence was with me. I could have passed out. I was praying, lost in prayer when I felt Him and heard Him speak affirming words to me. I was shocked." Divine restoration, body, soul, and spirit—that is the way of our Lord.

Christina

# See Your Jericho Moment

*"Now when Joshua was near Jericho, he looked up and saw a man standing in front of him with a drawn sword in his hand. Joshua went up to him and asked, 'Are you for us or for our enemies?'"*
*-Joshua 5:13*

*"Then the Lord said to Joshua, '**See**, I have delivered Jericho into your hands, along with its king and its fighting men.'"*
*-Joshua 6:2, emphasis added*

*"Then they came to Jericho. As Jesus and his disciples, together with a large crowd, were leaving the city, **a blind man**, Bartimaeus (which means 'son of Timaeus'), was sitting by the roadside begging. … Jesus stopped and said, 'Call him.' So they called to the blind man, 'Cheer up! On your feet! He's calling you.' Throwing his cloak aside, he jumped to his feet and came to Jesus. **'What do you want me to do for you?' Jesus asked him**. The blind man said, 'Rabbi, I want to see.' 'Go,' said Jesus, 'your faith has healed you.' Immediately he received his sight and followed Jesus along the road."*
*-Mark 10:46, 49-52, emphasis added*

*"Jesus entered Jericho and was passing through. A man was there by the name of Zacchaeus; he was a chief tax collector and was wealthy. He wanted to **see** who Jesus was, but because he was short he could not see over the crowd. So he ran ahead and climbed a sycamore-fig tree to see him, since Jesus was coming that way. When Jesus reached the spot, he looked*

*up and said to him, 'Zacchaeus, come down immediately. I must stay at your house today.' So he came down at once and welcomed him gladly."*
*-Luke 19:1-6, emphasis added*

Today in Jericho, there's a pile of rocks signifying the fall of the walls of Jericho for all the eager tourists passing through. I don't know when the pile of rocks was formed, but it makes you stop and think about the great victory for God's people that once took place. But for three specific men and scores of onlookers, Jericho was a place of deliverance and new frontiers, where people encountered Jesus. Blind eyes were opened, spiritually blind eyes received their sight, and Joshua encountered Jesus before the Israelites ever crossed over to take their ground!

The Lord simply mentioned the word "Jericho" to me one week. And with curiosity, I went on a treasure hunt and believe that the timing of Phil Wickham's song, "This is Our God," is a beautiful invitation for us to stand at the walls of impossibility we face right now and see Jesus. He's about to move in front of you, sword drawn, and arms outstretched. I want to shout this truth from the mountaintops: **God has not forgotten you, nor has He forsaken you. For the place where you are standing is holy ground.**

I want to speak to many of you because I believe God has a word for you to come and see Jesus right now over your 20-foot wall of impossibility with eyes that cannot see beyond your circumstance and your pain. He is speaking to the ones who are facing a health crisis, broken relationships, hopelessness, infertility, dashed dreams, and years of being completely stuck in cycles you cannot reverse. He is speaking to the ones who haven't been able to see the face of Jesus because all you can see is the mess and the grief and the pain through a lens of tears. He is asking you to stand up and get ready, just like He did with the blind beggar. In fact, He goes beyond just the need you are presenting and deep unto deep asks, *"'What do you want me to do for you (Mark 10:51a)?'"* What is it that you really need from Jesus today? Look up—He's standing in front of you with His sword drawn, leading the armies of the Lord on your behalf.

He has victory in store for the righteous, for this is why He died! His life meant your liberty and healing now and on the other side of this torn veil. Do we battle the realities of human error and a fallen world? Absolutely. But we also have a God who is familiar with our frailty and establishes the feet of His righteous ones. He fights for us, prays for us, and carries us in every detail of life. I have a brother-in-law in ICU from a stroke whom I am praying God does a miracle of mercy in and through. Human error and a fallen world have impacted this man of God, but if the Lord has not taken him home yet, we stand in the goodness and mercy of God over his life and call Heaven to Earth.

Beloved of the Lord, will you take hold of the words of this song today:

> "This is our God / This is who He is, He loves us / This is our God / This is what He does, He saves us / He bore the cross, beat the grave / Let Heaven and Earth proclaim / This is our God, King Jesus" -Phil Wickham, "This Is Our God"

**Your victory belongs to Jesus!**
**Your healing belongs to Jesus!**
**Your seeing belongs to Jesus!**
**Your future belongs to Jesus!**

These realities will only be the work of the Lord, but it requires your faith. You get to partner with the God of the universe and place your trust in His perfect response to your faith. He doesn't expect a field of faith, just a tiny mustard seed, as small as the comma in this sentence. But He wants you to walk to the walls of Jericho and trust Him as He leads you in this victory march. He wants you to get up when you hear His still small voice and come to Him in expectation. He wants you to climb the tree of your curiosity and face the opposition of your limits in order to encounter Him. He always comes in pursuit of us with an invitation that is very personal and intimate, only for you. His grace and mercy surround us as they did

Joshua, Zacchaeus, and the blind beggar as they walked into that space where Heaven touched Earth. All three guys needed to see Jesus. They needed to see God's goodness and the victory of Jesus in Jericho.

A change of course was required for all three guys in this town. They had to do something different to experience something different. And for each one, it was pretty outlandish. How do you tell a blind beggar to go to Jesus when he can't even see Him to find Him? Why would marching and shouting seven times around a city in lockdown release the hold on that city and cause it to collapse? Zacchaeus had to lay down his own dignity in that moment.

This was the counsel of the Spirit placed on my heart:

> I will come to My people in their despondency. I will call to them, and they will answer Me. They are seen by the Lord their God. I have taken up their cause, and **none are without hope**. My life covers sin and death. I have the final word over every matter, and My answer is not contingent on you; it rests on Me. In the same way Joshua overtook a fortified city, I will give the marching orders for victory. Get low and get dependent on Me, not on answers or self-sufficiency. Brilliant ideas and self-sufficiency won't work from here on out. What is ahead will require you listening only to My words. I am the One who overcomes for you, and I declare that you are an overcomer. By My blood and My testimony of who I say you are in Me, you will overcome. You will walk in victory and abundance. You will take the land I have assigned for you to take. Nothing will stop what I can do and will do for your good. My glory will be revealed in the Earth, and it's coming like a tidal wave. Get ready to be swept under. I have been waiting to release what is coming. Taste and see that the Lord is good!

This is your opportunity to stand in the place of your Jericho and see the Lord, who has come to meet you here. He comes to defend and to rescue and redeem with a righteous vengeance against your enemy. The blind will see, and the people of God will cross over into what He has promised for us before He returns. The place and time of history you are standing in is holy unto the Lord. See His sword drawn on your behalf—He is for you. His righteous ones belong to Him. Give a shout to these walls, in the name of Jesus, and watch them crumble in His presence and at His command!

Listen to this worship song: "This is Our God" by Phil Wickham

## TESTIMONY
### Jesus Pursued Me

After speaking at a meeting for her college organization, I met Emily, who wanted to know more about God. Over the next couple of months, we met and shared our lives. I learned that she gets most of her supernatural information from watching movies and television. As we talked about the spiritual realm, she explained she believed in the supernatural, but she wasn't sure how to navigate it because of the conflicting information in movies, television, and online. I told her I also believe in the supernatural, so we discussed what that meant.

Emily shared that she would lie awake at night, terrified of dying, going over every detail of her actions to make sure she could be right with God before going to sleep. I shared about how my relationship with Jesus gave me freedom and confidence in life and death. Slowly, we talked through Scriptures as I showed her how to have a relationship with the Father and confidence in her life and death. When I told her that this is possible by grace through faith in Jesus, I asked if she knew what grace was. Since she was unsure, I explained it, and her face lit up as she said, "I need to go call my sister!"

For several months, the free gift of forgiveness caused her to ponder grace and a relationship with Jesus, unsure if she could trust His grace and whether she truly wanted it. During the pandemic, she watched a film adaptation of the book of John. As she watched, the Spirit opened her eyes, and she realized that Jesus truly is the Son of God! All the pieces of our conversations over the past several months started to click together, and she decided to follow Jesus. The Lord, in His pursuit of her, met her exactly where she understood the world best: video.

Hannah

# To God be the Glory!

*"How beautiful on the mountains are the feet of those who bring good news, who proclaim peace, who bring good tidings, who proclaim salvation, who say to Zion, 'Your God reigns!'"*
*-Isaiah 52:7*

*"For we know, brothers and sisters loved by God, that he has chosen you, because our gospel came to you not simply with words but also with power, with the Holy Spirit and deep conviction. You know how we lived among you for your sake."*
*-1 Thessalonians 1:4-5*

*"On the contrary, we speak as those approved by God to be entrusted with the gospel."*
*-1 Thessalonians 2:4a*

*"'Now, Lord, consider their threats and enable your servants to speak your word with great boldness. Stretch out your hand to heal and perform signs and wonders through the name of your holy servant Jesus.' After they prayed, the place where they were meeting was shaken. And they were all filled with the Holy Spirit and spoke the word of God boldly."*
*-Acts 4:29-31*

*"For the Kingdom of God is not a matter of talk but of power."*
*-1 Corinthians 4:20*

*"For what is our hope, our joy, or the crown in which we will glory in the presence of our Lord Jesus when he comes? Is it not you? Indeed, you are our glory and joy."*
*-1 Thessalonians 2:19-20*

*"Dear friends, although I was very eager to write to you about the salvation we share, I felt compelled to write and urge you to contend for the faith that was once for all entrusted to God's holy people."*
*-Jude 1:3*

*"For to me, to live is Christ and to die is gain."*
*-Philippians 1:21*

In the spring of 2022, I returned from the Himalayan Mountain range where, glory to God, three unreached villages are now entirely reached with the gospel of Jesus! The wonder and power of Jesus is alive and moving to confirm the gospel message! He longs to perform His Word! The Word of God is true today, yesterday, and forever! His glory will cover the Earth, and the nations will come to know Jesus!

I have led teams all over the world, and never have I encountered a mix-up of travel due to just one delayed flight like we did. Satan was doing everything possible to hold us back from getting there because the Lord had gone ahead of us. There had to be a mighty spiritual war over that region that we were unable to see. Tucked away in the mountains of the Himalayas were three specific villages that were being prepared to receive the power, presence, and Person of Jesus! These three villages went from unreached to reached in just three days. Praise the Lord!

I want to tell you about a man who was blind and prayed to receive Christ in hopes of seeing again. My teammate, Maya, had shared the gospel and prayed for his eyes, and the Lord was working. My translator and I came up on their encounter, and she invited me to pray again for him. I got on my knees, anointed his eyes with oil, and a concert of prayer for his healing began. Jesus released His power right there on the porch of this home where a desperate man longed to see again.

Jesus, in His compassion, came and healed this blind man! News of the miracle spread quickly, and we got word that 20 families decided to follow Jesus as a result!

Let me tell you about another man, Darsh.* My translator and I walked up to him. Darsh was with two other men building his new home. He greeted us with a huge smile and eagerness. As we shared the gospel, the Holy Spirit was opening all of their eyes, and before Darsh prayed to receive Christ, he said these words: "There is coming a time when every person will receive Jesus." What was soon going to actually take place was most of Darsh's family was going to receive salvation!

As we continued down the road, we stopped in the yard where one of our team members, Caleb, had just led four men to Jesus. They wanted us to tell them more about Jesus—each so eager to learn about this Savior that they had just come to know. As we told them about Him being our perfect and final sacrifice, they were understanding more and more as the Holy Spirit was teaching them. They were getting perfect doctrinal revelation as we shared the Word with the Holy Spirit teaching them. As we ended the conversation, the oldest man among them said to us, "There is coming a time when every person will receive Jesus." My translator and I looked at each other wide-eyed because just 45 minutes earlier, Darsh said the same thing! The Lord was confirming His Word to us—we are in an era of harvest, Bride of Christ. The fields are ripe and need our beautiful feet to run to them!

Let me share one more story about two women. One was just two years older than me, and her daughter was 24. They invited us in for tea, and both couldn't stop smiling as we shared our message of hope. The husband was at school teaching, but his worker was there listening and peering through the slats of the wood in the other room.

We shared the gospel, and oh, how they longed to receive it! But if they accepted Jesus, or even gave us permission to pray for them, the husband would come home and beat both of them. That said, the mom needed healing in her back. As we left, she came and threw her arms around me, and I prayed, "Back, be healed in the name of Jesus." She said that they would sneak away on Sunday and go to the church. I know they could not confess with their mouths, but they believed, and I know Jesus will save them.

The enemy tried **everything** to keep us from getting to these villages. A simple agenda of three flights turned into three red-eye flights through three countries and then two more additional flights through South Asia. We experienced delays, setbacks, lost baggage (for the whole trip), and trials beyond our energy to endure. But Jesus had the final victory, and the great work He did in this team of nine is represented in the Scriptures above. Paul only had three weeks when he began the church in Thessalonica. We had three days to bring the people the gospel before we left. I believe that deep unto deep, God's purposes were accomplished in the mountains and in the lives of our team. He was fashioning us into a people who would contend for the gospel. Would we be those who go forward with nothing but the clothes on our backs? Would we be OK if all our comforts were removed and our plans delayed? Would we be OK if the Lord allowed us to face trials of many kinds so that the testing of our faith would make us mature and complete, not lacking anything?

My challenge to us, as I ponder the takeaways from my Himalayan journey for the Bride of Christ, is threefold:

1. Would we be willing to forsake life as we know it to take the gospel to those who don't know Jesus yet?
2. Will we be a forerunner who Jesus would choose to be prepared to help the Bride of Christ endure under fiery trial and still advance the gospel forward?
3. Would we ask the Lord to restore the joy of our salvation so that we would overflow with good news to everyone we meet?

> "The Lord is calling some to embrace a season of rigourous preparation to prepare others for the greatest transition in history, the return of Jesus." -Mike Bickle

My friend, Wade Aaron, wrote a 50-day devotional and activation book, "The Reward of the Lamb: A Journey of Discovering How to Walk Like Jesus." It's time to stretch out and learn to share Jesus and pray for miracles!

I pray that these days of intimacy and preparation get us ready to partner with Jesus to bring Heaven to Earth. I pray that we will be bold as lions and move with deep love and compassion for people. I pray for you to have a heart for the world Jesus so loves and yet be willing to forsake a love of the world that would sideline you and keep you entangled. I pray that His Spirit will fall on you like fire, and you will preach the Word boldly as you move with power. Sisters, it's time to get our beautiful feet shod with the gospel of peace and run with ferocious faith together!

*Names have been changed for security purposes.

Listen to this worship song: "My Testimony" by Elevation Worship

# TESTIMONY

## A Miracle in South Asia

My team was sharing the gospel in a home in South Asia when a man came in requesting prayer for healing. He experienced high blood pressure and dizziness and was unsteady when walking. We knelt beside him, looked into his eyes, and asked if he believed Jesus could heal him. He said, "Yes," so we proceeded to pray. Afterward, we asked how he felt, and he had the biggest smile on his face. He said he felt better, so we asked him to stand and see how he felt. As he stood, his walk was steady. He said the dizziness was gone, and his legs felt stronger as he believed Jesus had healed him. After we prayed for him, we went outside, and his son was there, also asking for prayer. He had problems with his liver and lungs and general achiness throughout his body. He said he believed, in Jesus' name, that he could be healed. When we finished praying, he took a deep breath and was breathing easier. We believe in faith that God was healing his internal body as well.

Becky

DAY 20

# Look at Us!

*"One day Peter and John were going up to the temple at the time of prayer—at three in the afternoon. Now a man who was lame from birth was being carried to the temple gate called Beautiful, where he was put every day to beg from those going into the temple courts. When he saw Peter and John about to enter, he asked them for money. Peter looked straight at him, as did John.* ***Then Peter said, 'Look at us!'*** *So the man gave them his attention, expecting to get something from them.*

*"Then Peter said, 'Silver or gold I do not have, but what I do have I give you.* ***In the name of Jesus Christ of Nazareth, walk.'*** *Taking him by the right hand, he helped him up, and instantly the man's feet and ankles became strong. He jumped to his feet and began to walk. Then he went with them into the temple courts, walking and jumping, and praising God. When all the people saw him walking and praising God, they recognized him as the same man who used to sit begging at the temple gate called Beautiful,* ***and they were filled with wonder and amazement*** *at what had happened to him."*

*-Acts 3:1-10, emphasis added*

These were ordinary, unschooled men who had spent time with Jesus and trusted in God's authority, and miracles broke out, salvation came by the thousands, and bound men were set free! That's the radical life of Christ in us! It's time we move in this reality with the assurance that Jesus breaks ground ahead of us.

Let's zero in on Peter's words: *"'Look at us! ... In the name of Jesus Christ of Nazareth, walk' (Acts 3:4, 6)."*

Peter and John gave the man exactly what he needed because they knew exactly what they had to give him: the manifested power of Jesus. We have come to rely on the wealth and provision of the Church to solve the needs of mankind. We invite others to come to church for benevolence, food, and, sometimes, good counsel for living. But do people come in their destitution to receive the power in the name of Jesus from your lips? Does His name have the ability to break strongholds of poverty? Yes. Does His name have the power to resurrect dead things to life, something gold and silver never could? Yes. So why have we gotten so comfortable directing people to our wealth and resources rather than the power of Jesus?

I received report that a blind man who was healed from his blindness in South Asia on one of our trips brought nine more families to the local church that was started after our time there. We didn't empty our pockets for this man; we brought him the power of Jesus. And because of the power of Jesus being evidenced in one life, a whole village is encountering Him. They are turning to Jesus as entire families because of the power of Jesus!

*"... and they were filled with wonder and amazement at what had happened to him."*
*-Acts 3:10b*

The question we must beg to ask is, how did Peter and John go from an understanding of their salvation to the demonstrative manifestation of the power of God through them? What catalyzed such faith? How was it that this very Scripture evidenced the resurrected Christ through these simple apostles: *"Everyone was filled with awe at the many wonders and signs performed by the apostles (Acts 2:43)"*?

Let's go back to a critical moment when Jesus prophesied what we would look like and what we would do: *"'But* ***you will receive power when the Holy Spirit comes on you****; and you will be my witnesses in Jerusalem,* *and in all Judea and Samaria, and to the ends of the earth (Acts 1:8, emphasis added).'"*

Peter and John knew they did not need to have physical resources to manifest the power of God for healing and deliverance. They just needed to **move** in His power. They needed to let it flow from their lips to the man in need. In confidence that Christ would come through, they commanded the man to fix his eyes on them: *"'Look at us!'"* If Jesus promised that they would receive power, then there was no need to doubt, question, or resist. It was time to respond to that promise!

Are you confident to say to the one who is stuck (emotionally, mentally, physically or spiritually), "Look at me"? Are you confident to say to the one who is blind (emotionally, mentally, physically, or spiritually), "Look at me"? They have nowhere else to look and nowhere else to receive the power of Jesus when God intersects them with **you**. That is your moment to show them the life of Christ that has been deposited in you for their awe and wonder! Church, we have to stop sending them elsewhere or telling them to look here or there. It's time we say to the lost and destitute and dying, "Look at me because I am going to bring you Jesus!"

> "In one moment, on the day of Pentecost, the Church stopped being a ragtag prayer huddle in an obscure upper room. Suddenly from Heaven, they became a global force supervised by an invisible person who was at once enveloping the world with conviction and serving as commander in chief of the armed forces of the Body of Christ on Earth. And doing it with all the power God the Father had given to Jesus." -Mario Murillo, "Vessels of Fire and Glory"[25]

*"'You killed the author of life, but God raised him from the dead. We are witnesses of this. By faith in the name of Jesus, this man whom you see and know was made strong.* ***It is Jesus' name and the faith that comes through him*** *that has completely healed him, as you can all see.'"*
*-Acts 3:15-16, emphasis added*

The pressure is off for us as believers in Christ to perform this power, but the pressure is on to conform to it! We don't get a pass on this life of Christ that lives in us for the sake of the world! We can't afford to say, "Come to my church," and hope people will encounter Jesus. That's our calling and our assignment. **We** get to bring them a powerful encounter with the Lover of their souls!

> "Live with a holy sense of urgency, as if today could be your last. Jonathan Edwards, a pastor God used to fuel a Great Awakening in the church, wrote in his resolutions that he would recite every day, '*Resolved*, To think much, on all occasions, of my own dying, and of the common circumstances which attend death.' … you and I need to remember that our homes and our health and our bank accounts and our vehicles and our jobs and our comforts in this life guarantee us nothing in this world. One day (and it could be today) they're all going to be gone, so we need to remind ourselves to live today for what lasts forever." -David Platt, "Something Needs to Change: A Call to Make Your Life Count in a World of Urgent Need"[26]

There is power in the name of Jesus to set captives free and open prison doors. There is power in the name of Jesus to heal the sick and comfort the brokenhearted. There is power in the name of Jesus to manifest His wonders and miracles through sons and daughters who have availed themselves to the love of God and the ministry of Jesus. I beseech you, in this hour of urgency, to live for Christ and let His power and His life overflow through you.

> "The same Peter who denied Jesus now spoke with boldness and led thousands into repentance and salvation through Jesus. It is impossible to be Spirit-filled and live apathetically. There is an overflow that will come as you

> allow the Holy Spirit to consume you. Your 'dry season' is over. Jesus says that you shall live in *overflow* … . This is the life God has for you, a life of overflow. God wants to fill you with His Holy Spirit to spark wildfires everywhere you go!" -Jessi Green, "Wildfires"[27]

Brothers and sisters, let His power flow through the very name of Jesus on your lips. These are your greatest days, and like the crippled man or the crowds, you, too, will watch with awe and wonder at what God is about to do!

Listen to this worship song: "That's the Power" by Hillsong Worship

# TESTIMONY
## Bellagio Healing

Four people from Canada were hanging outside of the Bellagio in Las Vegas, Nevada, watching the water show when they saw me carrying the cross. One lady asked, "What are you doing with the cross?" I told her that I was carrying it for the Lord. Then I offered to pray for healing. They all needed healing in their bodies. I prayed for different things including pain in their face, hands, and knees. The lady with pain in her face said, "My face feels relaxed." The hand pain lady said, "I feel tingly," and the knee pain lady was stunned because, after we prayed for her twice, she was totally healed. Her knee pain that was at level eight was now at zero. Each one had an encounter with the Lord by the Bellagio water show. I shared the gospel with them. They were not ready to accept Jesus, but they each had an encounter with Him that day.

Wade

# Scattered

*"'But you will receive power when the Holy Spirit comes on you; and you will be my witnesses in Jerusalem, and in all Judea and Samaria, and to the ends of the earth.'" -Acts 1:8*

*"On that day a great persecution broke out against the church in Jerusalem, and all except the apostles were scattered throughout Judea and Samaria. Godly men buried Stephen and mourned deeply for him. But Saul began to destroy the church. Going from house to house, he dragged off both men and women and put them in prison.*

*"**Those who had been scattered preached the word wherever they went**. Philip went down to a city in Samaria and proclaimed the Messiah there. When the crowds **heard** Philip and **saw** the signs he performed, they all paid close attention to what he said. For with shrieks, impure spirits came out of many, and many who were paralyzed or lame were healed. So there was great joy in that city." -Acts 8:1b-8, emphasis added*

Jesus is faithful to fulfill His words! He is faithful to perform what He speaks over your life. He is faithful to what He commissions over your life! Hold onto these two Scriptures while we walk with the disciples through their shaking and dispersing.

It's profound to me how much Jesus knows our propensity for hiding in comfort. He knew that in the midst of a politically charged environment—the harsh rule of Rome and the assault on the new believers of the way—they needed a place to hide. Stephen, a man of God, had just been stoned to death, and then Saul dragged people from their homes and put them in prison. I wonder whether what our Canadian, Chinese, Afghani, North Korean, African, and Indian brothers and sisters (to name a few) are experiencing today is a picture of the infant Church. Jerusalem's atmosphere was filled with weeping, fear, frailty, faith, and **expectation**.

My dear friend Joy texted me recently, "Jesus didn't say *'Come, follow me (Matthew 4:19a)'* to have us go sit in a church and do NOTHING." Sometimes it's easier for us to stay in our holy huddles and get comfy. We chew on the fat, get super full, and put our feet up. We simultaneously delight in His presence and our safety. What was true about the church in Acts 1:8 and Acts 8:1–8 is still true about us today. And as we watch the world heating up and persecution increasing, we have to get up, get out, and go. It's time to retract the footrest of our recliners and go.

The floodgates of persecution were released against early believers, just like it is today! According to Open Doors, in 2022, there have been:

- more than 360 million Christians living in places where they experience high levels of persecution and discrimination;
- 5,621 Christians killed for their faith;
- 2,110 churches and other Christian buildings attacked; and
- 4,542 believers detained without trial, arrested, sentenced, or imprisoned.

There are two meanings to the word "scattered" in this Acts 8 passage. The word denotes causing something to disappear like when scattering ashes. The other meaning relates to scattering seed through planting or sowing. This second meaning (in Greek) is what is used here. The precious lives of these believers were scattered seeds in all the places their lives landed. And while they went, they preached and demonstrated the gospel. The Lord used His people's persecution to scatter His Kingdom seeds! Their shaking from places of comfort caused the gospel to spread. If He's doing this all over the world, do you not think this will also include

American Christians? I do! The end result was for God's glory and the fulfillment of Jesus' words.

These accidental missionaries, who probably never thought they signed up for that job description, were now in full-time ministry. Is that any different for us today? If we carry the same commission today, do we get a pass? I don't think we do. So, we wrestle deeply with that! When I was prompted to pray for my server this week, I wrestled with my own comfort versus my obedience. I believe the Spirit is shaking the Church across the globe to scatter our lives as we go! The grace of this reality is that we don't have to be schooled, professional evangelists! We simply have to have open hands and a trembling yes before Jesus; that is all He needs in order to live His powerful life out through your surrendered life.

> "God wants you to use your words to honor His Name. More times than not you use your words to talk about your favorite sports teams, food, recent movies or tv shows, clothes and the list continues. The reason you talk about these things is that they are what you think about most. You can talk to just about anyone about these topics and yet not mention the way that Christ has changed your life. **If the Gospel has changed your life then talk to others about Christ. Even if it isn't the most elegant or if it's awkward, tell others.**" -Wade Aaron, "The Reward of the Lamb"[28], emphasis added

Hearing and seeing the miracles that Phillip did brought great joy to the city in which he served. The signs and wonders confirmed the gospel message. They went hand in hand! Many times, it's the miracle and wonder that opens the door for the gospel message. Jesus knows most intimately what that person needs to receive at the time of the encounter. We don't get to decide that; Jesus does. I can tell you from these moments of ministry that when Jesus does something so wondrous and miraculous, great joy accompanies those moments. When you pray for healing and it doesn't immediately come, don't lose heart! Read this testimony from my friend Wade:

> "Jesus even placed the gift of healing in the list of commands when preaching the Gospel for those that believe. As you pray for healing keep your prayer simple and tell the sickness go and then get the person to check it out. You may pray one or more times. There was an encounter where I prayed for an atheist to be healed nine times. Each prayer was simple and to the point and I had him check for a difference each time. On the ninth time, he was totally healed. He was stunned. The first eight times nothing happened that we knew of but he allowed me to pray each time saying, 'nothing is going to happen' but finally he got totally healed then I was able to share the Gospel with him. Be sensitive to the Holy Spirit in these moments." -Wade Aaron, "The Reward of the Lamb"[29]

My prayer for us over is that our craving and our courage would hit new depths and new heights in our lives. It's time to break our holy huddles. We must lock arms and run into that harvest field, considering all in our lives as nothing except knowing Jesus and partnering with Him to bring Heaven to Earth. We don't know how much longer we have, and the only thing we are bringing to Heaven with us is people. Can we so forsake our dignity, self-preservation, and comforts to bring people Jesus? Will you pray this prayer with me from the depth of your heart?

Jesus, help me to forsake me to talk about You. Help me throw off self-protection and self-preservation when it comes to speaking Your name or praying for people. I pray that You would infuse me with a fresh craving for You and a new level of courage to go as a scattered missionary like the believers in Acts. Take this surrendered life today and bring Yourself glorious joy!

Listen to this worship song" "Worthy of My Song" by Maverick City Music, featuring Phil Wickham and Chandler Moore

## TESTIMONY
### Nerve Pain Gone

For 15 years, I have struggled with chronic Lyme disease. Even though my body has been at its healthiest the last couple of years, I still deal with daily fatigue, achiness, and occasional neurological symptoms that manifest in nerve pain, muscle twitching, and numbness and tingling in my hands and face. Usually, these symptoms can be managed with sleep, proper diet, and rest.

When I knew God was calling me to go on a mission trip to South Asia, I gave Him my yes, but I had apprehension about how my body would handle the physical activity, lack of sleep, and stress. Two weeks before departure, I had a neurological flare-up with severe burning and itching in both arms, and I feared I would not be able to go. I recognized this as an attack from the enemy, so I filled my heart and mind with God's Word, knowing that since He had called me to go, He would give me the strength to do all that was needed.

As soon as I arrived at the airport for our departing flight to South Asia, my nerve pain was gone. Even with the lack of sleep, constant exercise, and dietary changes, my symptoms have not returned. I believe God healed my body, and He is continuing to do a healing work. Praise be to Jesus for His healing hand, not only in the people of South Asia while we were there but in allowing me to bring a miracle home in my own body.

Becky

# Wide-Open Spaces

*"After these things Jesus went away to the other side of the Sea of Galilee (or Tiberias). A large crowd was following Him, because they were watching the signs which He was performing on those who were sick. But Jesus went up on the mountain, and there He sat with His disciples. Now the Passover, the feast of the Jews, was near. So Jesus, after raising His eyes and seeing that a large crowd was coming to Him, said to Philip, 'Where are we to buy bread so that these people may eat?' But He was saying this only to test him, for He Himself knew what He intended to do. Philip answered Him, 'Two hundred denarii worth of bread is not enough for them, for each to receive just a little!' One of His disciples, Andrew, Simon Peter's brother, said to Him, 'There is a boy here who has five barley loaves and two fish; but what are these for so many people?' Jesus said, 'Have the people recline to eat.' Now there was plenty of grass in the place. So the men reclined, about five thousand in number. Jesus then took the loaves, and after giving thanks He distributed them to those who were reclining; likewise also of the fish, as much as they wanted. And when they had eaten their fill, He said to His disciples, 'Gather up the leftover pieces so that nothing will be lost.' So they gathered them up, and filled twelve baskets with pieces from the five barley loaves which were left over by those who had eaten." -John 6:1–13, NASB*

The people were making their annual pilgrimage to Jerusalem because the Passover feast was near. They would have been reflecting on how the Lord fed the Israelites manna in their 40 years in the wilderness following Egypt. People were quite curious about this Jesus and the healing miracles they were hearing about. Curiosity caused them to press in a little closer.

His love for them wooed them to a wide-open space where He could rest them in green pastures to restore their souls and feed their empty spiritual bellies. He would feed them in their own little wilderness that day, both literally and spiritually. John shares how they had been listening to His teaching all day and were hungry. Knowing what He wanted to feed them, He invited His beloved disciples to get hungry, too.

That morning, a mom had sent her poor, young son out with a packed lunch of barley cakes and two salted fish to be eaten as a relish on his cake. (Barley in that day was a very undervalued grain.) To feed thousands of men, women, and children seemed impossible to Philip. One thing was true of Jesus while He trained His disciples: He always positioned them against impossibility to show them the vastness of His power. As Jesus starts up his new catering endeavor that day, His guys look on with practicality, unbelief, and impossibility—so they thought.

The people didn't know the miracle was happening, but the disciples did. They got to partner with Him to distribute the miracle to the people! Later, their very lives would be a miracle of salvation—a salvation to be distributed to a waiting world. The precious Bread of Life was showing them how to partner with God to bring Heaven to Earth. They were learning what it would mean for the Bread of Life to be broken for the salvation of the world. Not one piece would be wasted. But here's the differentiator: **Jesus invited His disciples to come in close to observe what thousands and thousands didn't have the privilege to intimately see. He wanted to stir up in them a hunger for the impossible and miraculous.**

As I sat with Jesus, I asked Him to unwrap the significance of this story to me. I wrote in my journal the Holy Spirit's counsel regarding this text. This is what He placed on my spirit:

> Gather the hungry ones and let Me create a testimony that combines encounter and miraculous stories, a place characterized by My extravagant power and goodness.

Sit in the open space of My promises and My Word (a place of rest and quiet waters), and I will feed My hungry ones. I long for My people to get still and get hungry so I can come in joyous wonder and miraculous power. I will instruct My disciples (those following Me intently) on the hidden treasures, the behind-the-scenes that no one else sees, so that their faith goes even deeper. This is the privilege of following so closely to Me in the unknown. I will teach and train you how to partner with Me so intimately.

There are two audiences in this story: the wide-eyed disciples and the hungry crowd. Both needed to see, taste, and know I was the Bread of Life. Both audiences needed an encounter but at two different levels. Both needed to see the miracle, but only a few had the privilege of knowing the miracle's intimate details. Others just received the fruit of the miracle. Every person with eyes on Me has either option in an encounter—to be changed by the intimacy of being close or just receiving a meal.

The disciples saw what I did when presented with a need. They heard what I prayed for when given so little to work with. They got to walk through a test of belief and have faith strengthened within them. They got to feed the hungry people. They got to watch people go from being hungry to being full. They were participants in unlocking the miracle for the crowd.

What was impossible before was transformed into possible when it passed through Me. When confronted with the invitation to consume Me with their whole life, many fell away at that moment. Some would no longer follow Me. It was too much to accept, too much change. They wanted their feast with no responsibility to follow Me. Some just wanted to stay a part of the crowd—the

> onlookers—who would never get intimately close to Me. But I was the Bread of Life for both.
>
> I want people to experience the intimacy of My wondrous love and miracles. But it costs you something to stay intimately connected. You have to stay so close to Me to really see what I am doing. For some, it costs too much, and they just want to remain part of the crowd and go back home to life as usual. Where are My disciples who will stay so very close to Me?

Can't you hear Jesus' voice of longing that we come in close and see what others never will? Can't you picture His beaming smile and look of expectation? He has so much if we just come in close and get hungry for Him. This is His plea to us today. Will you take Him at His word as He invites you to see what others never will because you are so near to Him?

You can hear His heartbeat race when He sees the person across the way who He wants to love through you. You can feel His compassion rise up in you when He wants to bring miraculous healing to the person at the grocery store, and He wants to do this through your partnership with Him. The closer we stay, the more miraculous encounters we get to watch and participate in as Jesus partners with us and lives His glorious life out through us.

> Lord, I pray You would rest us today in the wide-open spaces of Your promises and Your wonder. I pray that we would come so close today to feast on our Bread of Life. Thank You for breaking Your very life for us that we would be whole, healed, saved, and set free. Thank You for not wasting any of the broken pieces of our lives but instead using them to testify about Your goodness, love, wonder, and power. Consume us as we make space. Clear the clutter and come close. We are ready!

Listen to this worship song: "We Make Space" by Melissa Helser

# TESTIMONY
## Hindu Priest Finds Salvation

Deep in the jungle of South Asia, in an unreached village of 99% Hindus, I sat with the chief priest of the local temple. He looked to be in his late 70s, very thin yet feisty in spirit. After days of hiking, my translator and I came to his house. I began to interact with him and ask about his life and beliefs. He was boasting in the power of his gods and wanted to hear nothing about the one true God. I could sense our time with him was not going to be fruitful for even planting a seed in his heart, so we decided to continue on. He was clearly not a person of peace.

As we walked, I spotted an old woman basking in the sun on her roof. We called her to come down to speak with us. As we started to share the gospel, she began speaking in circles. As I paused the conversation, I turned to see the old Hindu priest enter the room, carrying marijuana from his field. He told my translator I needed to smoke it, and it would give me peace. The translator spoke back to the man, "She is a doctor, she knows what that is." His eyes widened in surprise. "If she is a doctor, can she help me? My knees and back are in much pain." I knew this was an opportunity for God to show this Hindu priest His love and power. I said to the man, "I know that God can heal you and show you how powerful He is!" I asked him to sit down so I could pray for him in the name of Jesus. He was both compliant and curious.

The man sat, and I prayed for his knees and back to receive healing. He stood up and began to walk around and squat low to the ground. The pain was gone! None of his 33 million gods could have brought the healing he was looking for. The woman sitting with us saw the miracle of healing and asked, "Will you pray for my back and knees? I am in pain as well." We laid hands on the woman and prayed, and she, too, was completely healed. What happened next was the most extraordinary.

This miracle of healing opened both of their hearts to receive the one true God as their Lord! Both prayed to receive Jesus as their Savior that day. Then we learned that the woman we were sitting with was the wife of the old priest. Salvation came to their household, and both will now spend eternity with Jesus.

> *"I came to you in weakness with great fear and trembling. My message and my preaching were not with wise and persuasive words, but with a demonstration of the Spirit's power, so that your faith might not rest on human wisdom, but on God's power." -1 Corinthians 2:3-5*

Dr. Alex

# The Faith of a King

*"In the Lord I take refuge. How then can you say to me: 'Flee like a bird to your mountain. For look, the wicked bend their bows; they set their arrows against the strings to shoot from the shadows at the upright in heart. When the foundations are being destroyed, what can the righteous do?' The Lord is in his holy temple; the Lord is on his heavenly throne. He observes everyone on earth; his eyes examine them. The Lord examines the righteous, but the wicked, those who love violence, he hates with a passion. On the wicked he will rain fiery coals and burning sulfur; a scorching wind will be their lot. For the Lord is righteous, he loves justice; the upright will see his face."*

*-Psalm 11*

It's believed that Psalm 11 was written when David was running for his life from Saul. This king was pursuing his threat to the throne and was filled with all the rage of Hell. He was after David in order to destroy him. The counsel around him looked on with human reasoning and told him to flee and to run for his life, but David knew something different! David knew who had the final word over his life and where his ultimate protection came from. It would not come from mountains or hiding places; it would come from the very presence and person of God.

Fear was not the answer for David; he had to fix his faith on the One who loved him and called him. There was a destiny over David's life that the enemy wanted to snuff out. But God faithfully stood with David as his refuge and stronghold, his rock and fortress (Psalm 18). God fulfilled the purposes for David's life because He loved him. From this shepherd's fields to the throne, in moments of failure and humanity, God did not leave his side. This knowledge was the strength of David's life, and the Lord was formulating a faith in him to believe Him and hold onto His faithfulness even at the infancy of his calling. All of his days, God trained him in this truth until he saw him face-to-face.

*"In the Lord I take refuge."* This was David's opening declaration of Psalm 11 and essentially the opening declaration of his life. And then he reminded himself, when the counsel of his fear-mongering friends surrounded him, where God was. As all the fear and chaos ensues, where is God in the midst of it?

God is in His holy temple, seated on His heavenly throne (Psalm 11:4). He is not moving; He is not distant. He laughs at His enemies as He reigns in power. His faithfulness goes before Him. And, in fact, He sets a table for us in the very presence of our enemies (Psalm 23:5). So why would one flee in fear? God has victory in store for His righteous ones!

David's confidence was in an all-powerful, omniscient God. When the question was posed to David, "'*... what can the righteous do (Psalm 11:3)?*'" he shifted His gaze to the supremacy of God over earthly matters, human reasoning, and the power of fear. He began to see from Heaven's perspective. I love the words of the Passion Translation here:

> *"Yet Yahweh is never shaken—he is still found in his temple of holiness, reigning as King Yahweh over all. He closely watches and examines everything man does. With a glance, his eyes examine every heart, for his heavenly rule will prevail over all."*
> *-Psalm 11:4, TPT*

In this time of history, when we are seeing the very foundations of our nation, churches, and culture being destroyed and sifted, it's easy to look on in fear and wonder where we can flee. But Jesus calls us to see the One who is enthroned, who holds the final word of victory, who has defeated sin and the grave, who never leaves us nor forsakes us, who awakens us each morning with new mercy and exorbitant grace, who looks upon His righteous ones with a love that the human experience cannot quantify nor contain. **He is seated, having finished His work on the cross, and nothing we can do adds to any dimension of His love or sacrifice.** It is finished, and it is ours for all eternity. There is no height or depth in all of creation that can make us escape the very love and mercy and grace of God. His judgments for the righteous were paid on the cross. Oh, what a Savior! Oh, what an abundant inheritance we carry as kings and priests!

David stood at a crossroads between the counsel of fear and the faithfulness of God. It's the same crossroads where we are standing in our nation at this hour. Will we look to the One who sits enthroned in Heaven, or will we look at our small perspective and question the goodness of God in the land of the living? Is He worthy of our gaze and affection when He doesn't answer as we've asked? Or when our foundations seem to crumble under the schemes of wicked people? Is He still worthy of our trust? He is. He is, indeed.

One day we will stand face-to-face with the One our hearts adore. But until then, we hold to the promise that the pure in heart will see God (Matthew 5:8); He lifts His countenance upon us (Numbers 6:26), and we will see His face in righteousness (Psalm 17:15). There are encounters with Jesus for us that answer these promises as we walk in intimacy with Him. He is not distant but is the very breath we breathe and the essence of who we are as He dwells inside of us.

Beloved of the Lord, it's our hour to appropriate the faith He has given to each one of us, in order to cross over in complete trust. Our enemy may be facing us, and our hearts may feel weak and fragile; but even still, you are hidden, and you are seen by the Lover of your soul. So, take your abundant inheritance and **go**. Go to the streets and to the places where God's presence is void and bring His authority. Heal the sick, cast out demons, and preach that the Kingdom of Heaven is near. He is with you, and He is for you. His faithfulness will be your shield and rampart (Psalm 91:4)! You are a king and a priest in the Earth, so it's time, Church, to walk and minister like one!

*"Now therefore, thus shall you say to My servant David, "Thus says the Lord of hosts: 'I took you from the sheepfold, from following the sheep, to be ruler over My people, over Israel. And I have been with you wherever you have gone, and have cut off all your enemies from before you, and have made you a great name, like the name of the great men who are on the earth.'""*
*-2 Samuel 7:8-9, NKJV*

Listen to this worship song: "Faithful to the End" by Bethel Music, featuring Paul and Hannah McClure

## TESTIMONY

### Jesus Set Me Free

Over the years, healing prayer has been both complicated and painful. The Lord has healed me from alcoholism, fibromyalgia, arthritis in my hands, neuromas in my feet, panic attacks, anxiety, and fear. I still have degenerative disc disease and pain that has not yet been healed, and I have prayed for a lot of people who have not been healed. But I remain steadfast in my belief in healing prayer and in Jehovah Rapha, "God our Healer," that His ways are higher. I choose to believe He heals, I minister hope and healing to others, and I thank Him daily for my healing from addiction. He has given me a sound mind, and I praise Him that the battle in my mind ended in 2013 when He set me free!

Shannon

# Carriers of Mercy

*"They went across the lake to the region of the Gerasenes. When Jesus got out of the boat, a man with an impure spirit came from the tombs to meet him. This man lived in the tombs, and no one could bind him anymore, not even with a chain. For he had often been chained hand and foot, but he tore the chains apart and broke the irons on his feet. No one was strong enough to subdue him. Night and day among the tombs and in the hills he would cry out and cut himself with stones. When he saw Jesus from a distance, he ran and fell on his knees in front of him. He shouted at the top of his voice, 'What do you want with me, Jesus, Son of the Most High God? In God's name don't torture me!' For Jesus had said to him, 'Come out of this man, you impure spirit!' …*

*"He gave them permission, and the impure spirits came out and went into the pigs. The herd, about two thousand in number, rushed down the steep bank into the lake and were drowned. …*

*"As Jesus was getting into the boat, the man who had been demon-possessed begged to go with him. Jesus did not let him, but said,* ***'Go home to your own people and tell them how much the Lord has done for you, and how he has had mercy on you.'*** *So the man went away and began to tell in the Decapolis how much Jesus had done for him. And all the people were amazed." -Mark 5:1-8, 13, 18-20, emphasis added*

A storm preceded this encounter, directing the boat carrying Jesus and His disciples to an inlet on the lake. It was a rocky place where a wounded man was crying out for deliverance. His Heavenly Father heard His cries of desperation and sent Jesus across the lake to bring this one freedom. And this one would bring the testimony about Jesus' victory to an entire region!

The mercy Jesus showed this man compelled him in his desire to stay with Jesus. Can you imagine the peace and comfort he received in that moment when he encountered the peace and presence of Jesus? He had been known all over that region for being a powerful demon-possessed man. I wonder how many forgot his real name. I wonder how old he was when the legion of demons found their home in this man. What was the trauma that became an entry point? When his demons weren't manifesting and causing him to rage and hurt himself, can you imagine how ostracized, forsaken, forgotten, and alone he must have felt? God knew, and He sent Jesus across the lake for this one forgotten man.

That one moment with Jesus changed everything. He was seen for the first time in probably a very long while, and then he was set free. The whole herd of pigs paid the price that day, sadly enough, but even Jesus showed mercy to the demons by granting their request. Interesting thing to ponder, isn't it?

> "Demons cannot live in a person without something to 'feed' on. Something always will be in the person that gives the demons a right to be there. As I have mentioned before, demons are like rats, and rats go for garbage. Demons usually attach themselves to emotional or spiritual problems." -Charles Kraft, "Defeating Dark Angels"[30]

However these demons found an entrance into this man, Jesus knew his road back to healing and recovery would be in the context of his community where he was once known. He needed to belong, be received, and be welcomed back. Perhaps it was more healing for him to be with his family again than with Jesus and His disciples. That's not the case for every one of Jesus' disciples, but it seemed to be the case for this one.

Maybe someone would apologize for the rejection he experienced so he could move on in freedom!

Perhaps as the freedman walked home, this was his prayer:

> "Lord, I believe you are God with great purposes. You placed me into my particular family in a particular place in a particular time in history. I don't see what you see, but I ask you to show me, Lord, the revelation and purposes you have for me in your decision. I do not want to betray or be ungrateful for what was given to me. Yet at the same time, help me discern what I need to let go of from my past and what my essential discipleship issues are in the present that must be addressed." -Peter Scazzero, "Emotionally Healthy Spirituality"[31]

Whatever embrace he may have received, this man was compelled to share his testimony all over the Decapolis. The Decapolis were 10 Greek cities on the southern and eastern sides of the Sea of Galilee. Jesus commanded this man to go and bear witness in this predominantly Gentile region. His life change was so enormous that scores of people began to get curious about this Jesus. His mission field was no small task!

Christ lives in us, and, therefore, we are carriers of mercy to afflicted, suffering, outcast, sinful, and outrageous people. Jesus went out of His way that day to get this man free and running his destiny. You and I have the same privilege and calling with people who live and look nothing like us.

> Jesus, give us compassion for the ones You see that no one else sees. May Your life and grace and mercy flow out of us to demonized people in rocky crags and ornate beautiful homes. They are all around us and are crying out for someone to help set them free. Would You send us, Jesus?

Listen to this worship song: "A Love That Remains" by Bryan McCleery

## TESTIMONY

### My Own Encounter

On a recent trip to Latin America, my team of three headed to the home of a young woman who shared the same characteristics as this demon-possessed man mentioned in Mark 5. Her mother would often lock her in a room when her demons manifested because she was known to run through the hills with a machete and try to hurt people. Our church leader asked if we would pray for her. She was the family outcast, although young, tender, and beautiful. She sat on a stool as we prayed all we had learned to pray, for freedom from demons.

I know Jesus heard our prayers that day. I believe He sent us right to her. But the one thing I walked away with (besides a raging headache) was the possibility that we can do more damage to one another in our afflictions than any demon could do. The mockery, rejection, isolation, and humiliation from family members and other villagers seemed to accomplish much more than even a whole legion of demons in this woman's life.

Julie

DAY 25

# I Saw the Lord

*"Mary Magdalene went to the disciples with the news: 'I have seen the Lord!' And she told them that he had said these things to her."*
*-John 20:18*

Mary was ready! She went to the place she supposed Jesus was and looked eagerly. The angels met her that Easter morning. I can see Jesus telling the angels, "I've got it from here." Mary needed Jesus, and Jesus wanted His Mary.

**Her heart was positioned in desperation for the One she loved, and her feet were standing on the threshold of encounter.**

Throughout Scripture, we see those who saw the Lord. They encountered Him with their ears and their eyes. They needed to see Him just as we need to see Him. He faithfully came and revealed Himself to them without fail. In Job's, Gideon's, Haggar's, and Isaiah's despair, He met them in that place and brought them heart revelation of who He was and who He wanted to be to them.

**Their commissionings for the remainder of their days came from these very personal and intimate encounters!**

*"'My ears had heard of you but now my eyes have seen you.'"*
*-Job 42:5*

*"She [Hagar] gave this name to the Lord who spoke to her: 'You are the God who sees me,' for she said, 'I have now seen the One who sees me.'"*
*-Genesis 16:13, clarification added*

*"When Gideon realized that it was the angel of the Lord, he exclaimed, 'Alas, Sovereign Lord! I have seen the angel of the Lord face to face!'"*
*-Judges 6:22*

*"'Woe to me!'" I cried. "'I am ruined! For I am a man of unclean lips, and I live among a people of unclean lips, and my eyes have seen the King, the Lord Almighty.'"*
*-Isaiah 6:5*

Mary had the rest of her purposed life before her that had already been written for her. This tomb encounter was a new beginning for her. This encounter and the commissioning that ensued were imperative to her fulfilling the plans and purposes ordained for her before the foundation of the world. Mary's encounter at the tomb was a crucial part of her commissioning for the next chapter of her life. She would be key for the faith of the early church as she was the first one commissioned to preach the resurrected Christ.

**Mary's seeing was vitally important for the disciples to be able to see for themselves.**

The disciples were hiding in fear, but Mary was searching for the One she loved. His powerful presence catapulted her in, so much so that she ran to tell the guys that she saw Jesus. That fresh and deep revelation and conversation provided faith and preparation for Jesus' appearing to them. This passage from 1 John could have been the testimony of Mary when Jesus was believed to be dead and buried!

*"That which was from the beginning, which we have heard, which we have seen with our eyes, which we have looked at and our hands have touched—this we proclaim concerning the Word of life. The life*

*appeared; we have seen it and testify to it, and we proclaim to you the eternal life, which was with the Father and has appeared to us."*
*-1 John 1:1-2*

I want to see with my spiritual eyes and hear with my spiritual ears. But sometimes, we need to discern what we are seeing in the natural in order to pick up what God is speaking and showing us behind the scenes. Search for treasures hidden in secret places. I don't want to be blind, deaf, lazy, or distracted in this hour. I want to know the times and the seasons like the men of Issachar (1 Chronicles 12:32). When John "*was in the spirit (Revelation 1:10)*" alone and ready for an encounter, the Lord unwrapped the entire book of Revelation to him!

Go to the familiar places you have met with Jesus before. For me, it's a place in my home where the Lord has always met me and that He recently told me to go back to. He piqued my curiosity and expectation that He has things to share with me there. He is more eager to reveal Himself to us than we are hungry to receive it. Blessing comes with our hunger and desire for Him.

*"Then Jesus told him, 'Because you have seen me, you have believed;* ***blessed*** *are those who have not seen and yet have believed.'"*
*-John 20:29, emphasis added*

May these two passages be the cry of your heart in this season as we navigate the days ahead:

*"Take me away with you—let us hurry! Let the king bring me into his chambers."*
*-Song of Songs 1:4a*

*"I pray that the **eyes of your heart** may be enlightened in order that you may know the hope to which he has called you, the riches of his glorious inheritance in his holy people ... ."*
*-Ephesians 1:18, emphasis added*

At the threshold of a tomb or in an upper room of expectation, Jesus will show up. He always shows up wherever our longing hearts need Him. He responds to our hunger and our craving and our ache and our thirst. He's attentive to our cry. Let's go like Mary went—to the place she knew Jesus would be. Let's go with the expectation that we are going to encounter Him. Let's go in desperation for the One our hearts ultimately long for. And then let's pull up our dress, so we don't trip on the hem, and let's run and tell our brothers and sisters of the Jesus we have experienced and seen!

I bless you:

- with new hunger and desire for Jesus;
- to receive the revelation of His presence with you;
- to be changed in His presence;
- in the enlightening of your spiritual eyes and ears to see and hear at new depths;
- to have a mind that operates fully with the mind of Christ;
- to wait and not give up for your answer to come;
- with a fresh commissioning;
- with a tribe of passionate Jesus lovers you can lead;
- with faith to run to your brothers and testify with boldness;
- with joy in your encounters;
- with new wine and new oil!

Listen to this worship song: "My Soul Sings" by Jonathan David and Melissa Helser

# TESTIMONY
## The Miraculous Journey to Sight

A patient entered my office, burdened by the weight of a stubborn diagnosis—glaucoma. This patient, who we will call Sarah (to disguise her identity), had traversed the labyrinthine corridors of medical offices, deliverance sessions, and many healing prayer experiences, seeking solace in the expertise of countless doctors, specialists, and fellow brothers and sisters in Christ. Yet, despair clung to her like a shadow for none could alleviate her suffering.

As I listened to Sarah's tale, I knew that this encounter was no coincidence. Moved by an inexplicable force from the Holy Spirit, I decided to pray for Sarah, to intercede on her behalf. I closed my eyes and, beseeching the Holy Spirit, petitioned for her deliverance from the clutches of glaucoma and a spirit of *pharmakeia*. Two days passed, and Sarah called, her voice trembling with excitement. She had visited her ophthalmologist and undergone a thorough examination.

The ophthalmologist, astounded, delivered the extraordinary news—there was no longer any pressure behind Sarah's eyes, no trace of excess cerebral spinal fluid. The glaucoma, which had plagued her life, had vanished without a trace. It was an inexplicable reversal, defying medical logic and prompting awe in the hearts of those involved.

Sarah marveled at the power of constant prayer. The undeniable treatment plan of the Holy Spirit had unraveled the chains of disease and set Sarah free.

Sarah and I stepped out in faith and saw firsthand that the boundaries of human understanding are meant to be pushed, that miracles are not confined to the pages of ancient texts but continue to unfold in the tapestry of our existence. Miracles are not reserved for the chosen few but are accessible to all who dare to ask and believe.

Dr. Alex

# He's Closer Than He's Ever Been

*"... and* ***among the lampstands*** *was someone like a son of man, dressed in a robe reaching down to his feet and with a golden sash around his chest. The hair on his head was white like wool, as white as snow, and his eyes were like blazing fire. His feet were like bronze glowing in a furnace, and his voice was like the sound of rushing waters. In his right hand he held seven stars, and coming out of his mouth was a sharp, double-edged sword. His face was like the sun shining in all its brilliance."*
*-Revelation 1:13-16, emphasis added*

*"'Look, I am coming soon!* ***My reward is with me, and I will give to each person according to what they have done****. I am the Alpha and the Omega, the First and the Last, the Beginning and the End.*

*"'****Blessed are those who wash their robes****, that they may have the right to the tree of life and may go through the gates into the city. Outside are the dogs, those who practice magic arts, the sexually immoral, the murderers, the idolaters and everyone who loves and practices falsehood.*

*"'I, Jesus, have sent my angel to give you this testimony for the churches. I am the Root and the Offspring of David, and the bright Morning Star.'*

***"The Spirit and the bride say, 'Come!' And let the one who hears say, 'Come!' Let the one who is thirsty come; and let the one who wishes take the free gift of the water of life. ... He who testifies***

***to these things says, 'Yes, I am coming soon.' Amen. Come, Lord Jesus. The grace of the Lord Jesus be with God's people. Amen."***
*-Revelation 22:12-17, 20-21, emphasis added*

He's coming into view. There is a Light at the end of this tunnel in history, and we are running to the Light. What we always thought about Him (right and wrong), He's beginning to course correct. Our vision, our paradigms, and our perspectives are changing in the very light of His presence. We are going to see Him one day how He really is—in all of His beauty. But until then, He's committed to showing us who He really is in all truth, and it's beautiful! We get there by communing with Him and pressing in, in greater longing and deeper passion. I decree that even the Bride's worship is beginning to deepen as we come face-to-face with Jesus in this era.

> "Take a moment to ponder this. We were designed by God with the capacity to not simply commune with Him through conversation but be one with God—to share His thoughts and perceptions, to know His mind through His Spirit." -Shawn Bolz, "Encounter"[32]

This is the kind of communion He longs to have with us. A communion that is so deep, even our groanings don't have human words. It's the language of our heart to Father, Jesus, and Holy Spirit—the cries and desperation to take us deeper than we've ever gone. It's the cry in the midst of redemption that says, "Show me your face," because there is nothing else we long to possibly see. It's the times when we feel less connected and more distracted that we stop what we are doing to grab the hand of our First Love and come close.

When you look at history, He is closer than He's ever been to His return. Our hearts are crying, "Come, Lord Jesus, come." But on the flip side of this truth is the fact that when we begin to long for Him in new and fresh ways, He just seems closer than He's ever been. Maybe it's that our desires are changing. He's living in us, so He couldn't get closer. But do we really tap into this longing that lives inside of us? Jesus, who takes up residence in our lives, desires that we give Him more and more permission to make His life known in us and through us. The entire world is longing for us to find ourselves consumed with Christ in us, the hope of glory!

*"The entire universe is standing on tiptoe, yearning to see the unveiling of God's glorious sons and daughters! For against its will the universe itself has had to endure the empty futility resulting from the consequences of human sin. But now, with eager expectation, all creation longs for freedom from its slavery to decay and to experience with us the wonderful freedom coming to God's children. To this day we are aware of the universal agony and groaning of creation, as if it were in the contractions of labor for childbirth. And it's not just creation. We who have already experienced the first fruits of the Spirit also inwardly groan as we passionately long to experience our full status as God's sons and daughters—including our physical bodies being transformed."*
*-Romans 8:19-23, TPT*

One evening, my mom texted me out of the blue with a question: "Do you love the world?" I felt like I needed to have a strong biblical response but wanted to answer her honestly. I thought about how John 3:16 says, *"For God so loved the world … ."* And in 1 John 2:15, it says, *"Do not love the world or anything in the world."* So, which is it? Jesus had to love the world to bankrupt Heaven and come on an ultimate rescue mission for humanity. This can be the love that lives inside of us for a lost world. But a love for the things of the world that excludes Jesus is a misplaced affection. Our hearts have attached to things other than Jesus and need a course correction. The cords of loving kindness pull on our heartstrings, and repentance woos us back home.

We are getting ready! We are getting ready for history to shift when the Father hands Jesus His Bride. It's going to be a battle to the finish line—let's just all count on that. The enemy will pull out every tactic and throw every fiery dart. So, I implore you to gaze upon His beauty, let your heart become enraptured in His goodness, create space to commune and hear His voice, and avail yourself to His sanctifying and redemptive work in your life. I declare that your life has been purposed for **this time in history**. As my friend Jordan Gaudet said to me the other day, "Julie, I am so excited to be alive in this time!"

I want to tie this all together with a portion of a prophetic word from Patricia King that the Lord placed on her heart to share in her book, "A Prophetic Manifesto For the New Era."

> "This is an hour when hearts and the intents of the hearts will be revealed. It is an hour when I will separate good and evil, the holy and the profane, the flesh and the Spirit, the world and My Kingdom. It is a time of harvest when both the wheat and the tares will become evident. It is time to consecrate yourself afresh unto Me and My purposes, for you are in the world as My salt and light, but you are not of the world—you do not partake of its dark mindsets and deeds because you are My light and you represent My light. I am about to display a great wave of My authority and My great power, and I am looking for a people whose hearts are completely Mine. I am looking for those who are completely consecrated unto Me, for they shall partner with Me to display great moves of My power and presence in this era. They shall be humble, not looking for their own glory and renown but Mine alone. They are My consecrated ones. They shall perform My exploits so that the world may know that I AM. All My children are invited to walk with Me in this way. Many are called, but only those who consecrate themselves will be chosen for what I am about to do in the earth."[33]

He's closer than He's ever been. Can He look you eye to eye and say the same of you? Let's go. There's no time to waste; the world is standing on tiptoe, waiting for us to get there!

Listen to this worship song: "Hey Jesus" by Elyssa Smith, featuring Steffany Gretzinger

# TESTIMONY

## A Divine Intervention: A Life Saved by Miracles

Late one evening, I received a call from a patient who was seeking guidance. Against medical advice, the patient left the emergency room sensing that her symptoms were not adequately explained by the diagnosis of COVID-19. A deep knowing tugged at her soul, urging her to seek further assistance.

When I arrived at the patient's home, my instincts alerted me to the severity of the situation. I assessed her vitals and discerned a possibility of dehydration and decided to initiate intravenous fluids while investigating further. As I prepared the IV, the Holy Spirit urged me to pause and listen to the patient's lungs before proceeding. As I did, I realized there was more at play. As I listened to the patient's lungs, the Holy Spirit showed me the issue was pulmonary embolism. It was a grave and life-threatening condition requiring immediate attention.

I prayed fervently with the patient, invoking divine guidance and protection for the journey ahead. The patient was admitted to the ER, necessary tests were conducted, which confirmed saddle pulmonary embolism. The medical staff acknowledged that, had the patient been treated solely for COVID-19, her life would have been tragically cut short. The precise instructions given to me by the Holy Spirit had proven to be a lifeline.

This story reminds us that amidst the chaos and uncertainties, there exists a guiding force—a force that surpasses the boundaries of science and awakens our spirits to the extraordinary.

Dr. Alex

# A Special and Significant Encounter

*"Jesus entered Jericho and was passing through. A man was there by the name of Zacchaeus; he was a chief tax collector and was wealthy. He wanted to see who Jesus was, but because he was short he could not see over the crowd. So he ran ahead and climbed a sycamore-fig tree to see him, since Jesus was coming that way.*

*"When Jesus reached the spot, he looked up and said to him, 'Zacchaeus, come down immediately. I must stay at your house today.' So he came down at once and welcomed him gladly. All the people saw this and began to mutter, 'He has gone to be the guest of a sinner.'*

*"But Zacchaeus stood up and said to the Lord, 'Look, Lord! Here and now I give half of my possessions to the poor, and if I have cheated anybody out of anything, I will pay back four times the amount.' Jesus said to him, 'Today salvation has come to this house, because this man, too, is a son of Abraham. For the Son of Man came to seek and to save the lost.'" -Luke 19:1-10*

As intentional as Jesus is, I wonder if he passed through Jericho just for Zacchaeus, whom we will call Zac. Jesus was heading to Jerusalem for His triumphant entry and had become quite popular and admired. But there was one man the Father had sent Him to encounter in that city, and it was Zac.

Zac was a despised and rejected man, hated by the people because of his robbing the Jewish people by charging excess taxes and keeping the part not required by Rome. He didn't get wealthy from an inheritance. Zac recklessly stole from the people, and they couldn't stand him. But oh, how the Father loved him, and He sent Jesus to Jericho that day to rescue, restore, and redeem the life of Zac—to pull him from his own prison and set him free.

> "Time and again it is the morally disgusting, the socially reviled, the inexcusable and undeserving, who do not simply receive Christ's mercy but *to whom Christ naturally gravitates.* He is, by His enemies' testimony, the 'friend of sinners.' … But the dominant note left ringing in our ears after reading the Gospels, the most vivid and arresting element of the portrait, is the way the Holy Son of God moves toward, touches, heals, embraces, and forgives those who least deserve it but truly desire it." -Dane Ortlund, "Gentle and Lowly"[34]

Zac didn't hide in the shadows when he couldn't see Jesus. He didn't hang his head and go back home. His short legs had nothing on His overwhelming desire to truly see. No, he **ran** to this 40-foot fig tree that was in bloom, climbed like a little boy, and got up higher so he could simply catch a glimpse of this Jesus. They caught one another's eyes, and having never met, Jesus called him by name. Then in front of everyone, Jesus stated his longing to spend time with Zac at his house to share a meal.

**In the whole massive crowd, Jesus saw the one man—and He knew his name!**

Zacchaeus's name means "pure." Immediately, I thought of Matthew 5:8: *"Blessed are the pure in heart, for they will see God."* The Lord knew before the foundations of the world that Zac would encounter Jesus, and He would give Him a new heart. As determined as Zac was to get wealthy, he had the same determination for spiritual wealth as it was deposited in

Him by God. It just had to be redeemed! Zac wanted to receive the abundant wealth of God's Kingdom as a son. And Jesus knew Zac would be one who radically displayed His Kingdom. He was the least likely candidate in Jericho that day, or so he thought.

Zac had to fulfill a unique destiny that required a special and significant encounter that would mark Zac forever. He received Jesus that day, and salvation came to Zacchaeus. His repentance restored his character. Out of repentance came an immediate response to return everything he had taken and to make restitution. God did an impossible work in Zac's heart all because he had a face-to-face encounter with Jesus. And just like Zac, this is true for us:

> *"For he chose us in him before the creation of the world to be holy and blameless in his sight. In love he predestined us for adoption to sonship through Jesus Christ, in accordance with his pleasure and will—to the praise of his glorious grace, which he has freely given us in the One he loves." -Ephesians 1:4-6*

**There are no limitations put on us in order to encounter Jesus. If you want Him, come and receive Him!**

Today, He comes to you, spotting you sitting in place you maybe have never sat in before in order for you to catch His eye. It's an unfamiliar place to you but known by Jesus. He knew where you would be this day. And His compassion, love, expectation, and excitement lead Him to see you and spend the day with you. How He longs to recline with you at the table and teach you (like His disciples) how to lean back and receive from Him, how to feast at His table, and how to truly turn to the life He has for you.

We don't know what Zac did following the restitution to the people of all he had taken from them. Jesus knew that this wealthy man was repenting. I wonder if he helped take the gospel from Jerusalem when the Church was scattered in Acts. Did he live a life of radical generosity because of the grace and mercy shown to him that one day with Jesus?

The beautiful part of repentance is what God does with our turning. All of the ways the enemy sought to live his depraved life through ours, God turns and makes into a highway of righteousness for His purposes. He unlocks even greater authority to push back the kingdom of darkness in our lives. And then He releases His Kingdom through us because now we are fully aligned with His heart and purposes. There is more to the fruit of repentance than just confessing sin, turning back, and doing life differently. The gates swing open wide so the King of Glory can come running through your life!

Zacchaeus may have been a wee little man, but he had the faith of a giant that day! Father God was ready to put a ring and robe on his son after he came down from that tree. And I believe an entire city was impacted by this one personal encounter. Jesus needed to see only one man in Jericho that day, because an entire city would encounter the love of God through Zac's new life!

Listen to this worship song: "Rescue" by Lauren Daigle

# TESTIMONY

## My Special and Significant Encounter

Having been diagnosed with scoliosis during my teen years, I had to wear a Milwaukee brace to stretch my back during the growth process, preventing further curvature until I was fully grown. This brace was a metal, atrocious, bulky, and uncomfortable eyesore that started from the chin and attached to a plastic mold around my hips. Not only did the brace restrict movement, but it also attracted many stares. I was only allowed to take it off for one hour every day in order to take a shower. The brace helped, but the doctor told me I would always have back trouble and have difficulty when pregnant.

When I went to college, I met Jesus as my Lord and Savior. At the same moment, I met the Holy Spirit and power! My life was abruptly turned upside down, and it wasn't long before I met God as Jehovah-Rapha, the Healer.

I was invited to my first women's meeting at a home in Baton Rouge, Louisiana. The minister was a fiery, elderly lady who approached me and asked if she could measure my legs. We discovered that one leg was shorter than the other, and when she began to pray, we watched my leg grow out until both were even. I was already 5'8" so in my mind I was thinking, "God, don't you think I'm tall enough?" Within minutes my leg was free, my back straightened out, and I measured 5'10" tall!

God proved the doctor wrong! Subsequently, I have had eight pregnancies with no back pain ever!

Suzy

# Burning and Drifting

*"Now that same day two of them were going to a village called Emmaus, about seven miles from Jerusalem. They were talking with each other about everything that had happened. As they talked and discussed these things with each other, Jesus himself came up and walked along with them; but they were kept from recognizing him.*

*"He asked them, 'What are you discussing together as you walk along?' ...*

*"When he was at the table with them, he took bread, gave thanks, broke it and began to give it to them. Then their eyes were opened and they recognized him, and he disappeared from their sight. They asked each other,* ***'Were not our hearts burning within us while he talked with us*** *on the road and opened the Scriptures to us?'"*
*-Luke 24:13-17a, 30-32, emphasis added*

Can't you just feel the roller coaster of emotions these two guys felt? Three years with Jesus, then deep despair after His death. They decided to walk away from Jerusalem—the place where everything took place for them, the place where everyone was gathered for Passover, a time of reverence and remembrance. They walked out of town with all of that behind them. I can imagine deep grief and so many questions, perplexed, and feeling deep loss. I wonder if they were thinking, "Let's just forget it. The pain is too deep, and the questions too many. Let's just go."

**Jesus came to meet them on their road of pain.**

He could have gone to scores of people that day, but He chose to come to them to turn their hearts from downcast and drifting to being on fire with holy passion. They needed His presence and His words. Jesus knew they needed to see Him again. His appearing to them sent them running back to declare the truth and revelation of Jesus with their own lips and their own conviction.

I awoke with these two words in my mind: **burning** and **drifting**. To be honest with you, I feel the magnetic pull toward these two polar ends at times. My heart burns within me for Jesus—His presence, His goodness, His Spirit. Then at times, I get so sidetracked by the cares of the world, and I feel my perspective shift. How do we get to a place of continual burning? Is it possible? At the very core of these questions is desire—do we desire to continually burn with passion for Jesus? Or are we OK with seasons of burning and seasons of distraction and drifting?

Those two guys needed an encounter in the midst of their pain. They needed their Jesus. They needed to hear truth and remember all that they had seen. They needed to go back to Jerusalem with a testimony of having seen Jesus in risen form. Their testimony of declaration was part of their breakthrough.

When we are stuck in disillusionment, Jesus comes. He always comes.

There is a differentiator when, in our hearts, we are not following Him any longer. Drifting becomes the very thing that takes us far from Him. Scripture tells us that in the last days, even the elect will fall away. When Jesus returns, will He find our faith on Earth? Will we look like the rest of the world who has lost hope, bound and entangled by culture and the burden the enemy places on our shoulders? Will we see with spiritual eyes the battle for our passions and ask the Lord to consecrate our lives afresh for Him?

*"But you need to be aware that in the final days the culture of society will become extremely fierce. People will be self-centered lovers of themselves and obsessed with money. They will boast of great things as they strut around in their arrogant pride and mock all that is right. They will ignore their*

*own families. They will be ungrateful and ungodly. They will become addicted to hateful and malicious slander. Slaves to their desires, they will be ferocious, belligerent haters of what is good and right. With brutal treachery, they will act without restraint, bigoted and wrapped in clouds of their conceit. They will find their delight in the pleasures of this world more than the pleasures of the loving God. They may pretend to have a respect for God, but in reality they want nothing to do with God's power."*
*-2 Timothy 3:1-5a, TPT*

This is our culture and the days in which we are living. It can become disheartening and overwhelming. Our hearts can grow weary if we don't see Jesus coming to us in the midst of this to reignite our passion for Him. I have devoured Dane Ortlund's book, "Gentle and Lowly." I think it is one of my favorite books. In it, Ortlund writes of our compassionate Jesus, compelled toward us like He was compelled to come to his two friends on the Emmaus road.

> "Christ loved his own all the way through death itself. What must that mean for you? It means, first, that your future is secure. If you are his, heaven and relief are coming, for you cannot be made un-his. He himself made you his own, and you can't squirm out of his grasp. And it means, second, that he will love *you* to the end. Not only is your future secure, on the basis of his death; your present is secure, proven in his heart. He will love you to the end because he cannot bear to do otherwise. No exit strategy. No prenup. He'll love to the end—'to the end of their lives, to the end of their sins, to the end of their temptations, to the end of their fears.'" -Dane Ortlund, "Gentle and Lowly"[35]

I don't believe it's going to get easier from here on out. I think we are on a fast track to the return of Jesus. But I want to burn with passion from

Him and for Him because He is the most important Person in my life. He holds the Lordship and the highest place of honor in my life. I want to be so anchored in Christ that I am not prone to drift or walk away from where I walked with Jesus all these years. Will you pray this prayer with me?

> Jesus, will You consecrate me afresh today with a radical love and holy pursuit of Christ alone? Circumcise my heart and remove the little stones (the altars and idols) that are blocking the flow of living waters gushing from my life. Will You come and consecrate me today for what You want to do in and through my life? Lord, remove the things that are causing me to be distracted and drift. Holy Spirit, fall afresh on me, Your Bride, that I would burn with holy passion, unwavering, laser-focused on Jesus, my finish line and great reward. Forgive me for wandering and for becoming distracted in this hour that I lose sight of the times in which I am living that are going to require focused faith and keeping short accounts with You all day long. Protect me from the evil one and from his plans and schemes to cloud my vision and take me into the captivity of activity. Will You set me free today to run my race, unhindered and uninhibited? Come and anoint me today that I may overflow with Your power and Your presence. In the powerful and merciful name of Jesus.

I prophesy to you that He is coming with fresh fire for you. Open your hands and receive it!

Listen to this worship song: "Rest on us" By Maverick City Music and UPPERROOM, featuring Brandon Lake and Eniola Abiove

# TESTIMONY
## Bones Grow Back

My husband, Doug, was trying to fix something on the lawnmower and accidentally stuck his hand in the power mower blades. I drove him to the hospital emergency room. A team of doctors and nurses immediately took him into surgery to repair three fingers that were severed and broken. They allowed me to stay in the room as they repaired his fingers by putting pins and sutures in them. We were told it would take several weeks for the hand to heal.

During a post-op visit six weeks after surgery, an X-ray was taken, which showed the ring finger bone was receding. After we got home, I placed my hands on Doug's hand, asking God to heal the bone in his finger and for the bone to grow back. A few weeks later, the X-ray showed the bone had grown back and his finger was perfectly normal. He has never had problems with these fingers. Jesus is so faithful. He is waiting for us to ask Him for healing—it's really just that simple!

Ev

# An Urgent Plea, Part 1

*"He said to them, 'Go into all the world and preach the gospel to all creation. Whoever believes and is baptized will be saved, but whoever does not believe will be condemned. And these signs will accompany those who believe: In my name they will drive out demons; they will speak in new tongues; they will pick up snakes with their hands; and when they drink deadly poison, it will not hurt them at all; they will place their hands on sick people, and they will get well.'"*
*-Mark 16:15-18*

*"'But you will receive power when the Holy Spirit comes on you; and you will be my witnesses in Jerusalem, and in all Judea and Samaria, and to the ends of the earth.'"*
*-Acts 1:8*

*"I came to you in weakness with great fear and trembling. My message and my preaching were not with wise and persuasive words, but with a demonstration of the Spirit's power, so that your faith might not rest on human wisdom, but on God's power."*
*-1 Corinthians 2:3-5*

As our team stood at the precipice of the mountain villages of South Asia, we declared the words of the song we started off with that morning. It became the anthem of our team as we shouted the name of the One who came to save and deliver them. I envisioned an army of angels crashing in on those villages, opening wide the gate so that the King of Glory may come in! And how did He come? He came disguised as hikers and moms, translators, doctors, businesspeople, missionaries, and daughters—Jesus, who was ready to proclaim the gospel in clarity and usher in the power and presence of the Holy Spirit. We get to partner with the God of the universe to bring the Kingdom of Heaven to Earth. There is no greater adventure, honor, or joy in all of life! As my teammate said to me as we were walking through the jungle, "This is really living!"

*"I have won them by my message and by the good way I have lived before them and by the miracles done through me as signs from God—all by the Holy Spirit's power. In this way I have preached the full Gospel of Christ all the way from Jerusalem clear over into Illyricum."*
*-Romans 15:19, TLB*

I cannot imagine the gospel preached without the Spirit's power making Jesus seen and known—in word and in the manifest power of Himself. They go hand in hand beautifully. This is the full scope of the gospel! We saw with our own eyes deaf people hearing and speaking, blind eyes opening, stroke patients moving, and people crying as the Lord delivered of them of pain and sickness they had battled for years. Jesus did it when He walked the Earth, and He does it again as He lives in and through us!

Everything Jesus did in those villages in South Asia He did to confirm His love and His goodness, to evidence the gospel message we were preaching. We bring our faith, praying with unction and conviction that God is good and freely leave the results to Him. We don't get to determine how or why someone is healed or not. We simply get to bring them our faith on their behalf and let God be God. But to know that some believe that God's miracles, signs, and wonders do not exist today is grievous to me.

> "Through the gospel, we all become ambassadors of Christ, reconciling the world back to God first and foremost by not counting their sins against them and then

> by demonstrating His love through allowing His Spirit to manifest through us. So instead of making evangelism only a message we preach, it becomes a life of love, showing people what God is like. We give to the world abundant life because that is what we have in Christ. ... Jesus wasn't just telling people about the goodness of God—He was showing it to them. And if we want to see the gospel advance in power wherever we are, we must be willing to imitate God, to walk in love, and to freely give what has been given to us." -Peter Louis, "Back to the Gospel"[36]

We are in a critical moment where the devil has captivated the imaginations of billions of people. From false religion, media, and movies (to name a few), he has been trying to hijack the attention of people. People are ultimately longing to encounter the power of the One who loves them lavishly and who died to set them free. Break any ties to the belief that Jesus doesn't heal or perform miracles so that you can minister in the power of the Spirit with fruitfulness, faith, and freedom, in Jesus' name.

There is a harvest ahead of us! Jesus is asking us to pray for this harvest and to ask Him to send harvesters. Jesus said how we would go about doing that in Mark 16:15-18. So, I must ask you these crucial questions: Will you be willing to be one to risk it all and to go before others and lead the way? Will you count the cost and go?

Are you willing to allow your theology to be wrecked by experiencing the impossibility of Christ? Will you allow Him to be God outside of the limitations of your experience so that the Kingdom of Heaven can come on Earth?

Will you make room in your heart for miracles whether you have yet to see any? Let's allow God to transform our faith to believe Him for everything—salvation unto eternity and the appropriation of the cross in these human bodies and souls of ours!

> "God still uses ordinary, run-of-the-mill individuals—men and women who abandon their lives to His will and make themselves available to His maneuvering. Jesus commanded every believer to join the Great Commission by making disciples of all nations. Some may enroll in this missional endeavor at home; others will go abroad. The location you serve at is not as important as your joyful obedience to God's global mandate. ... With William Carey's admonition in mind, I will ask you to lower me down into the goldmine of souls. Some of you will go with me as global Kingdom workers; others will stand on the ridge and hold the ropes while you lower us down. You and I are 'sent ones' called to live and thrive on mission today." -David Joannes, "The Mind of a Missionary"[37]

There is much at stake to have a theology steeped only in the mind, devoid of faith for miracles. In unreached people groups, wonders lead to belief. Now is the time; run with freedom into the plans and purposes of Jesus! No limitations. No stronghold of intellectualism devoid of power. Only zeal for the love of Jesus to be unleashed all over the world. You are called and sent for this purpose. Now go and make Him known in every way!

Listen to this worship song: "I Speak Jesus" by Charity Gayle, featuring Steven Musso

# TESTIMONY

## From Despair to Triumph: A Miraculous Healing Journey

This is the awe-inspiring story of a man serving a life sentence in prison, burdened by a relentless diagnosis, and the miraculous healing that ignited hope against all odds.

John (disguised patient name), a courageous soul, had traversed a treacherous path, battling the challenges that accompanied his HIV diagnosis. As the years passed, his treatment plan, though necessary, had taken a toll on his body. Kidney damage, bone deterioration, and fading vision cast a shadow over his spirit. Despite the tireless efforts of numerous doctors and specialists, the prognosis remained bleak and even more so now that he was dealing with these medical circumstances in federal prison.

In the face of adversity, John held onto faith. Daily prayers were lifted, beseeching the Lord to intervene, to heal his failing body, and restore his shattered hope. Yet, as time went on, the physical evidence seemed to contradict the fervent petitions that rose from his soul.

Amidst this ongoing struggle, a family friend had a divine encounter during a revival. Filled with an unwavering belief and guided by the Holy Spirit, she declared healing prayers over John, sensing an extraordinary intervention on his behalf. Driven by this revelation, she reached out to John's mother, becoming a beacon of hope in their lives.

One week later, the phone rang, and a voice filled with exultation pierced through the silence. It was John, rejoicing with newfound vitality, declaring that he had been healed by the Holy Spirit. His elation cascaded through the receiver, transforming despair into unrestrained jubilation.

John's specialist had visited him in the prison infirmary, and the verdict was a testament to the miraculous. The doctors' voices echoed in unison, proclaiming the inconceivable—a reversal of his ailments. The once-damaged kidneys had regained their vitality, his vision showed signs of improvement, and the knees that once screamed for replacement now found solace in restoration. Moreover, his HIV status revealed an undetectable presence, a testament to the power of Holy Spirit healing.

The news spread like wildfire among John's family, igniting a flame of hope in the hearts of those who had lost faith in John's healing and deliverance. John's story has become a testament to the resilience of the human spirit and the infinite power of prayer. It reminds us all that even when the road seems unending and miracles appear elusive, faith has the power to awaken the light of a new dawn and conquer the darkest of nights within a prison cell.

Dr. Alex

# An Urgent Plea, Part 2

*"He told them, 'The harvest is plentiful, but the workers are few. Ask the Lord of the harvest, therefore, to send out workers into his harvest field.'"*
*-Luke 10:2*

As I returned from taking a team of 12 to preach the good news in the most remote villages of this South Asia mountain region, my heart was stirred to a new level of deep compassion. I saw the Holy Spirit move as I have never seen in my lifetime, with scores of salvations and unfathomable healings and miracles. It was glorious, and the Lord poured out anointing on our team in a fresh way. We carried new wine and new oil with an even greater authority! But at the end of the fourth day, as we experienced significant suffering sitting with destitute and forgotten people, I wondered to the Lord, "How much longer can I do these trips?" My heart was breaking. I was all poured out, and the days were long with ministry. Demon-possessed people needed deliverance; spiritually dead people needed resurrection, and the physically broken needed healing. I have led six Extreme Teams over the past three years, but this one was in a space entirely of its own.

On that day, we followed the river to a village that only had access to the mainland for six months of the year. Otherwise, the river flowed so fiercely that people were unable to cross into other villages. That meant that in a medical emergency or food shortage, these people were stuck. The government refused to build a bridge to this community. The poverty was overwhelming to me that day. These people had nothing. They were stuck entirely and in every way.

There was not one believer there or anyone who cared to go there. After sharing the gospel with this village, we asked the locals if there was anyone sick we could pray for. They directed us to a paralyzed woman across the river. As a team, we decided that no one would come here again, so it was our opportunity to go and pray for her and bring Jesus to her.

After crossing the river, this was the sign of Christ to her village. She was considered just a "backward class" and discarded by the rest of society.

Upon reaching this paralyzed woman, we were undone by the level of rejection from her community. She was all alone to fend for herself. A thatched roof would not keep out the rain during the rainy season. Dirty brown water filled her drinking cup. She was fed scraps that no one wanted.

Positioned next to the stall of cows, she sat in utter hopelessness and despair, waiting and longing to die. One thing I do know—she never had eight Christians in her little hut praying for her and bringing her Jesus. **And in He came with the gift of her eternal salvation.** As we prayed and pulled Heaven down for her healing, we envisioned her running out of that dilapidated hut so that the entire village could be saved. God had a different plan, however, that we could not see in that moment.

We left knowing that His character is good and unchanging even though the paralyzed woman did not walk. One thing we know is that she went from death to life. God will always be glorified, for that is who He is!

> "The motive is this, 'Oh! that God could be glorified, that Jesus might see the reward of his sufferings! Oh! that sinners might be saved, so that God might have new tongues to praise him, new hearts to love him! Oh! that sin was put an end to, that the holiness, righteousness, mercy, and power of God might be magnified!' This is the way to pray; when thy prayers seek God's glory, it is God's glory to answer thy prayers." -Charles Spurgeon

We are faced with a grim reality in America as less than half of Christ followers know the Great Commission. Churches are moving further and further away from caring about a global mission focus. The Great American Dream is sweeping both the church and the culture. We are becoming more and more myopic in our viewpoint and less and less concerned with those around the globe who have never heard the name of Jesus. More than 3.4 billion people exist in the world today who have never heard of Jesus! How do we wrap our hearts and feet around this reality?

> "Today, many fallen aspects of culture impact the Christian mindset and permeate the Church at large. Our practices, judgments, and beliefs sway to social pressures, often giving way to the world's breed of groupthink.
>
> "Could this be one of the reasons why over fifty-percent of professing Christians do not know what the Great Commission is, why evangelism is going out of style, or why so few believers thrive on mission today? Or, more broadly, why so few answer the call of Christ to cross cultural, geographic, and/or linguistic boundaries to publicize the name of Jesus in foreign lands? After all, the collective social codes of behavior pay little respect to such radical expressions of love for Christ. ...
>
> "But when we downplay God's mission, our sight grows myopic, and our worldview becomes ethnocentric. We no longer see the expansive fields that are ripe and ready for harvest—either at home or abroad." -David Joannes, "The Mind of a Missionary"[38]

We are in a critical moment for the Bride of Christ. Jesus is setting a new normal before us where the Bride of Christ is going to naturally move in signs and wonders. This will confirm the gospel to those who need to experience the power and presence of Jesus. The gospel will be demonstrated and proclaimed in tandem with a mighty harvest waiting to be harvested. Intellectualism without wonder will be a thing of the past. But more must take hold of this reality and run to the harvest fields. We need more workers in the field! We need more to raise their hands and say, "I will do whatever it costs to take the gospel wherever God sends me." Jesus' prayer for more workers 2,000 years ago is just as critical now. I have seen it with my own eyes. There are people in places longing for a message of hope and salvation.

If we don't go, who will? If we don't tell them, who will (Romans 10:14-15)? If we have life, it is ours to give away, not hold onto in self-preservation. When I wrestled deeply if I could continue these Extreme Teams, the next day, my heart was undone. With every person I encountered, I had to fight back tears. I woke up that day crying tenderly in my sleeping bag and felt the Lord shifting my heart in even deeper compassion and compulsion. I must go. While I have life and strength, I must go.

My urgent plea is not only to my own heart but to yours as well. If you are reading this and you aren't in the grave, you must go, physically and/or spiritually. Workers need resources, and they need prayer. Each one of us can do something to get more workers in that harvest field! The days are urgent, and the need is compelling. Would you ask the Lord today to send you as a worker into His harvest field? Would you ask Him to reveal your part in fulfilling the Great Commission to the ends of the Earth?

> "At the culmination of the ages, people from every corner of the globe will be present before God's throne. What part will you play in ushering the nations into His throne room? Recognizing that praise from all nations is, in fact, the reward of Jesus' suffering, **are you prepared to do everything in your power to make Him known in the world?**" -David Joannes, "The Mind of a Missionary"[39], emphasis added

Listen to this worship song: "Good News" by Bryan and Katie Torwalt

# TESTIMONY
## Healed from Unrelenting Pain

In 1986, I fell down a flight of stairs and landed in excruciating pain with my right foot dangling off my leg. I had fractured my fifth metatarsal and torn five tendons. In those days, a plaster cast was the only thing done. It never healed correctly; I had major scar tissue. Then, in 2014, I stepped in a hole, injuring my right ankle again. I was given an orthopedic boot and it eventually healed, leaving me with chronic pain and instability.

A world renowned surgeon wanted to perform a brutal repair of my foot and ankle, which would result in four months in bed and six months of nonweight-bearing recovery then physical therapy with no promise of a cure. I declined and waited on God.

After waiting for years, in 2023, on a Zoom Bible study call, Dr. Alexandria Watkins was praying for a woman with a knee and toe injury. In the mid-dle of her prayer, I remembered what Dennis, a man of God, had spoken about Alexandria. He prophesied that she "would not only heal people in the physical realm but also in the spiritual realm." I rejoiced as I agreed with her prayer for my healing.

I had not been able to sleep for years because of the pain in my ankle, but that night was different because I didn't need medication to alleviate the pain. I was completely healed, over a Zoom call, while Alexandria prayed for the other woman. I have had zero pain or instability since. I thank God for this miraculous healing that has freed me from years of unrelenting pain!

Connie

# Is He Worth It?

*"In a loud voice they were saying: '**Worthy** is the Lamb, who was slain, to receive power and wealth and wisdom and strength and honor and glory and praise!'" -Revelation 5:12, emphasis added*

*"But Moses said to the Lord, 'Oh, my Lord, I am not eloquent, either in the past or since you have spoken to your servant, but I am slow of speech and of tongue.' Then the Lord said to him, 'Who has made man's mouth? Who makes him mute or deaf, or seeing, or blind? Is it not I, the Lord? Now therefore go, and I will be with your mouth and teach you what you shall speak." But he said, 'Oh, my Lord, please send someone else.' Then the anger of the Lord was kindled against Moses … ." -Exodus 4:10-14a, ESV*

Warning: This was not an easy devotional to write, nor is it an easy devotional to read.

The words of this devotional today were spurred on from this new worship song by Jesus Culture:

> "A yes to God is dangerous / But You're worth it / I'm all in / You're calling, calling / Here I am, I'm all in, all in / Take everything, You're worth it, worth it / Wherever You lead me, I will follow"

Is He worth it? It's the question of the hour. For many of us, it wasn't the question when we received salvation and the promise of eternity with

Him forever. But as Jesus moves in and takes more ground in our life, we are faced with this tough question: Is He worth it? One stone turned over at a time.

When He asks for more of our lives, is He worth it? When you scan the landscape of your whole life and all that has been entrusted to you, do these so-called treasures carry greater worth than Him? This is a question I am pondering and processing with the Lord as I look at the totality of my life. Is there anything or anyone in my life that holds more worth than Him?

> "Jesus is in every way a Bridegroom. That is why He is not satisfied with mere slavish obedience. He desires our heart, our total dedication. As our Bridegroom He asks, 'How much am I worth to you? How much are you ready to sacrifice for Me? For love of Me can you give Me your loved ones—children, parents, friends? Can you give Me your home and country if I ask for these? Are you willing to comfort Me in this way? Will you go anywhere I call you in order to save souls? Can you sacrifice your prestige, your strength, your longing to be loved, your deepest secret wishes—for love of Me?" -Basilea Schlink, "My All for Him"[40]

Let's just lift the hood on this, shall we?

Is He worth your vacation time to follow Him where He calls you to go? He was willing to give His life so the lost could come home. Could we give Him a week of our four weeks of vacation? What if He asks for all four?

Is He worth your finances? He has given you what you have needed. He has also supplied His people with abundance so we could expand the Kingdom. Do you spend it all on you, or have you followed Him into sacrificial love?

If your children want to become missionaries, is He worth it? They won't have high paying jobs, but they will follow Him to the ends of the Earth. Will you support that?

If He asks you to lay aside 30% of your income (instead of 10%) to build His Kingdom, is He worth it?

Is He worth getting rid of the busy in your life to pick up your calling and go with Him His way?

Is He worth keeping your vows you made to Him when you first fell in love with Him?

Is He worth "wasting" your time in His presence, to sit at His feet and become more like Him? Is He worth that? Or do Netflix, novels, and podcasts seem more rewarding and educating?

If He asked you to downsize your home to create margin and capacity in your life, is He worth that?

Is He worth your sobriety for a life of holiness and righteousness?

I would dare to estimate that the Church has been more resourced with provision right now than ever in history. And two paths lie before us—we either go or we send. There's not a third option as it pertains to the gospel of Jesus and the world He died for. We have all the resources to reach the world with the gospel, but somehow we also have a million reasons to spend and busy ourselves with everything else (known as the "captivity of activity"). It comes down to the question of our lives: Is He worth it? Or does everything else that brings us temporary fulfillment and pleasure take greater value? It's a heart issue, and I'm looking at my own heart as I write this to you. And quite honestly, it's causing repentance to rise up in me.

I was recently asked to go to a country in the Middle East that is not the safest of all the places I could go. My husband was a little taken aback but was emphatic that I need to go. Is my life so precious to me that it's worth preserving, or is my obedience to Jesus more important? (Tough question!) If I were to die for the gospel, is He worth it? Or is my safety and family and my self-preservation more important? We have to wrestle deeply with these things because they will either hold us back or free us to run with faith and focus.

One day we are going to be on our faces before Jesus, crying out with all of Heaven, "Worthy is the Lamb." We will sing it with our entire being.

Why are we waiting for Heaven to declare His worth when we can worship Him now in our sacrifice, obedience, and faithfulness? If we don't believe He is worth it now, we will store up barns of treasures, live for today and not eternity, and waste all He has placed in your hands on earthly endeavors rather than Kingdom exploits.

Lord, turn it all around. Take our finances, our vacation time, our spending, our priorities, our desires, our homes, our occupations, our families and turn it around. Don't let us waste our lives living for us, Jesus. Unravel our heart priorities, and counsel each one of us today to be all in, nothing reserved and nothing held back. When You call us like You called Moses and we have a list of great excuses why we need to say no, Lord, don't back down. Move Your people into radical faithfulness in this hour so the world will have an encounter with Jesus!

> "Love is costly and requires more than mere kindness. Jesus was not just a first-century do-gooder whose ultimate aim was to spread good cheer and congeniality. Rather, he announced himself as the Way, Truth, and Life. He compelled his followers to live life in light of eternity, submitting to his kingdom's righteous standards. He called for and required complete surrender to God's will, and demonstrated true sacrifice when he 'moved into the neighborhood' to offer himself as the payment for humanity's sins. We dare not dumb down the cost of loving God and loving our neighbor. It cost Christ his life. Shall it cost us any less?" -David Joannes, "Gospel Privilege"[41]

Lost people are begging for a dying chance to experience Jesus and just don't know it, and **you** are the one to bring it to them. Why? Because He is worth it. Lose your life, Church, so you can pick up the greater thing. We have little time left. No more excuses. He is worth it!

Listen to this worship song: "All In" by Jesus Culture and Brett Lee Miller

# TESTIMONY
## A New Heart

My extended family has such an extensive list of heart issues that doctors are researching our specific heart issues for medical reports. Several relatives have pacemakers, and, unfortunately, several others have died prematurely.

About 20 years ago, I started getting extremely tired. When I tried to exercise, my heart would go into tachycardia, and I would feel like I was going to faint. I called one of my cousins to discuss this because, even though she was younger, she already had a pacemaker. She informed me that fatigue was a sign that my heart was failing. Therefore, I made an appointment with a cardiologist. After wearing a heart monitor for a month, he diagnosed me with atrial fibrillation, mitral valve prolapse, and tachycardia. He prescribed beta blockers and said I'd eventually need a pacemaker.

After picking up the medication from the pharmacy, I returned home, planning to take the first dose. But when I looked at the pill container, I decided not to take any. I received a surge of faith and said to myself, "I'm not taking this medicine. God is going to heal me!"

Three months later, at a women's retreat, the minister said, "God's going to heal someone's heart." As I walked to the front of the room for prayer, I realized no one needed to pray for me. I felt God go into my heart and either fix it or give me a new one. It hasn't skipped a beat from that day forward.

Eventually, I went back to the cardiologist, and he put me through two days of extensive tests. When he walked into my waiting room with the results, he declared, "Your heart is perfect!"

Suzy

# Immovable Resolve

*"From Peter, an apostle of Jesus the Anointed One, to the chosen ones who have been scattered abroad like 'seed' into the nations living as refugees in Pontus, Galatia, Cappadocia, and throughout the Roman provinces of Asia and Bithynia. You are not forgotten, for you have been chosen and destined by Father God. The Holy Spirit has set you apart to be God's holy ones, obedient followers of Jesus Christ who have been gloriously sprinkled with his blood. May God's delightful grace and peace cascade over you many times over!*

*"Celebrate with praises the God and Father of our Lord Jesus Christ, who has shown us his extravagant mercy. For his fountain of mercy has given us a new life—we are reborn to experience a living, energetic hope through the resurrection of Jesus Christ from the dead. We are reborn into a perfect inheritance that can never perish, never be defiled, and never diminish. It is promised and preserved forever in the heavenly realm for you!*

*"Through our faith, the mighty power of God constantly guards us until our full salvation is ready to be revealed in the last time. May the thought of this cause you to jump for joy, even though lately you've had to put up with the grief of many trials. But these only reveal the sterling core of your faith, which is far more valuable than gold that perishes, for even gold is refined by fire. Your authentic faith will result in even more praise, glory, and honor when Jesus the Anointed One is revealed.*

*"You love him passionately although you did not see him, but through believing in him you are saturated with an ecstatic joy, indescribably sublime and immersed in glory. For you are reaping the harvest of your faith—the full salvation promised you—your souls' victory!"*
*-1 Peter 1:1-9, TPT*

Peter is the one man mentioned second to Jesus in the Gospels. He's a man whose life consisted of failure and zeal, unbridled courage, victory, fear, and great faith. He knew what the cost of following Jesus looked like, and he knew how it felt to need to be reinstated by Jesus. His past didn't define his calling, but it sure shaped it. Grace became the foundation of Peter's life. And in the midst of persecution and suffering, he called this baby church to even more, no matter the cost.

On the shores of Galilee as a young fisherman, Peter was called by Jesus to begin a life of impossibility. He was commissioned on the beach by Jesus in Luke 22:32, TPT: "'*But I have prayed for you, Peter, that you would stay faithful to me no matter what comes. Remember this: after you have turned back to me and have been restored, make it your life mission to strengthen the faith of your brothers.*'" At Pentecost, 3,000 people were saved as the words of Christ were declared through Peter's lips. In partnership with the power of the Spirit, this man turned the world upside down. And historians record that he was even crucified upside down on a cross. He carried the gospel power, wrapped in the reformational message of grace, to the places God assigned for him. He held back once and never did it again. His life was marked for the sake of the gospel to the very end.

In these nine verses, look at what we have been given in Christ!

- We are the chosen and destined ones of God.
- We are temporary residents in a foreign land.
- We are set apart as His Holy ones; holiness is our inheritance.
- He had foreknowledge of us, enwrapped in His omniscience, fully known.
- We are gloriously covered by His blood and made clean.

- Grace and peace are ours for the taking!
- We have extravagant mercy for this journey called life.
- We have a new, living, energetic, extravagant hope.
- We have been reborn and given an incorruptible inheritance that is eternal.
- We are kept by the power of God, and our salvation is secure.
- He has given us the gift of faith to hold on to until Jesus comes.

These things are true of us, and yet trials will come! Our faith will be tested as we go because it is so precious to the Lord!

> "Our faith isn't tested because God doesn't know how much or what kind of faith we have. It is tested because *we* often are ignorant of how much or what kind of faith we have. God's purpose in testing is to display the enduring quality of our faith. … If gold is fit to be tested and purified by fire, then how much more our faith, which is far more precious than gold? God has a great and important purpose in testing our faith." -David Guzik, 1 Peter 1 commentary[42]

Peter could go back and strengthen the church because of what he walked through. He could call up the faith of that infant church because he knew the grace and mercy and love of Jesus so deep inside of himself. There was a resolute conviction in his bones that he testifies to in the pages of his letters.

Peter had a choice to take his boat back out and take up fishing after Jesus left, persecution ensued, and the believers were emotionally on the fritz. He could return to what he knew, and I presume Jesus would call and commission someone else. But Peter was so compelled by the love of God that he was willing to risk it all for the sake of the gospel. Jesus was worth the persecution. Jesus was worth the sacrifice. Jesus was worth Peter's very life. Do we have the same level of conviction? Are we wrapped tightly enough in our identity as daughters, called ones, chosen ones, commissioned ones, marked and sealed ones? There's a burning in my heart for us to live out the rest of our days so utterly convinced of His love for us that come persecution, suffering, rejection from friends, etc., we are immovable in the love of God, burning for Him until He comes for us.

That's revival. This is jubilee.

> "Everything about God is extreme in the best possible sense. He is infinitely good, infinitely holy and powerful, infinitely beautiful, magnificent, and glorious. These are just a few terms to describe Him. But none of the endless lists of traits and characteristics confine Him. Religion, which I define as *form without power*, tends to attempt the impossible task of restricting Him into neat little packages, giving us a false sense of intelligence and ultimately control. But He is bigger and bigger and bigger still. Each virtue gives us a glimpse into that which is beyond measure but is open for observation. You could take one trait and explore it for all of eternity but not come close to exhausting the depths of who He is in that particular virtue." -Bill Johnson, "God is Good"[43]

If your faith is being tested right now, I want to pray a prayer of immovable resolve over you.

> Father, I pray that in Your infinite goodness and intimate power, You would fortify my sisters. I pray that, like Peter, we would overflow with conviction, by the power of the Holy Spirit, to love You passionately, no matter what it costs. I pray that we would be anchored in Your love, tethered so tightly to Your heart, and operating with the mind of Christ, that each test becomes a confirmation of Your goodness. Each place of faith that is refined in the

fire will bear forth the glory of God in their lives. I declare that in Jesus' name. I pray for strength and steadfast immovability in her innermost being today, Lord. And I pray that joy would come in the morning; the joy of the Lord that is her strength. Fill her mouth with praise and her eyes with seeing Your hand moving things on her behalf. I pray for the gift of faith to increase, not decrease in this season, in the name of Jesus! Amen!

Listen to this worship song: "Jubilee" by Maverick City Music featuring Naomi Raine and Bryan and Katie Torwalt

# TESTIMONY
## Testing of My Faith

I remember a time when I metaphorically took my shoes off in following Jesus. I was disillusioned, distraught, and foundationally questioning the love of God because I couldn't see His hands of mercy in my pain. And it was not long after I knew I was being called by the Lord to radical faith that the testing came.

One December, we were on a snowy, desolate road in Oregon headed to a sledding hill. The girls were little, and we had faced one delay after another to get on the road that morning. At every turn, we were detoured no matter what we did. As we were driving, the snow began to fall, and the road required snow chains for us to proceed. We pulled up behind another driver who had also stopped to put chains on his tires. My husband, Mike, got out of the van and began speaking to the man from the other car.

As I looked up, I saw my dear friend, Melissa, running to my car. She was my roommate in Santa Barbara during my senior year of college. She had endured a lot in her life, and we had lost touch for some time. I looked at her face and knew that God had miraculously and intimately moved Heaven and Earth that day for me to see and be embraced by Melissa. I knew if God cared that much about the details of my life on that day, on that random road in Oregon when we had traveled from Texas and she had come from California, I could trust Him.

The next morning, I told the Lord that I would get my shoes back on and I would follow Him no matter what. I decided in my heart and in my will that He was trustworthy, no matter the depth of my faith that was being tested.

What I thought was a delay became an encounter with the intimate love of Jesus.

Julie

# Follow Me

*"After John was put in prison, Jesus went into Galilee, proclaiming the good news of God. 'The time has come,' he said. 'The kingdom of God has come near. Repent and believe the good news!' As Jesus walked beside the Sea of Galilee, he saw Simon and his brother Andrew casting a net into the lake, for they were fishermen.* ***'Come, follow me,'*** *Jesus said, 'and I will send you out to fish for people.' At once they left their nets and followed him. When he had gone a little farther, he saw James son of Zebedee and his brother John in a boat, preparing their nets. Without delay he called them, and they left their father Zebedee in the boat with the hired men and followed him."*
*-Mark 1:14-20, emphasis added*

*"Then he called the crowd to him along with his disciples and said: 'Whoever wants to be my disciple must deny themselves and take up their cross and* ***follow me****.'"*
*-Mark 8:34, emphasis added*

*"****Jesus looked at him and loved him****. 'One thing you lack,' he said. 'Go, sell everything you have and give to the poor, and you will have treasure in heaven. Then come,* ***follow me****.'"*
*-Mark 10:21, emphasis added*

*"'Come,* ***follow me****,' Jesus said, 'and I will send you out to fish for people.'"*
*-Matthew 4:19, emphasis added*

*"My sheep listen to my voice; I know them, and they* ***follow me.****'"*
*-John 10:27, emphasis added*

I was speaking to a group of women in Virginia, where we had just launched a new Arise chapter. There was a woman in her late 20s sitting in the center of the room. She looked at me with eyes of longing. I had a sense in my spirit that God was calling her into full-time ministry. As we spoke afterward, she shared with me that she has been hungry to find a group of women who care about the Great Commission and taking the gospel to the lost. With tears in her eyes, she shared the dryness of the season she had been in because the Church doesn't seem to care about this anymore.

Her assessment is accurate. Some states have scores of women who have lives centered on the gospel. Other states have a mere handful, but the remnant of the people will usher in the harvest!

**Will you be a part of the remnant of Jesus in this hour who is wide-awake, desperate for Him, and positioned to carry His purposes in the Earth?**

If we look at the responses of the first disciples of Jesus, we see the phrase "at once" defined all their dispositions (except the rich young ruler). They were willing to leave vocations, social norms, families, relationships, and familiarity to follow Him. The invitation from Jesus rested on their hearts, which manifested in their feet.

We are reaching a critical crossing over for the Bride of Christ as she walks toward her Bridegroom and the wedding of the Lamb. We are racing against time, so I write this with a heart and passion for urgency! On one hand is the promise that we will be made ready for His return. On the other hand is the mantle of urgency that Matthew 28:18-20 steers us toward. Go, therefore! If we have all we need in Christ, what we have received in our hearts needs to drop to our feet. It's time to move! We follow Him exactly where He always went—to the lost sheep. We don't get to give ourselves an out, saying, "That's not my gift," "It's not my stage of life," or "I'm too busy." In the same sense of ownership that the first apostles in Acts received, we, too, are marked and commissioned to this time in history and to the nations of the world. More than 3.4 billion have yet to hear the name of Jesus. We must follow Jesus and go!

**Does Jesus have permission to change anything and everything in your life? Does He have permission to change your vocation, your friend group, your social life, your place of residence, and even your worldview?**

Americans battle something that no one else battles in their worldviews, and that is the American dream. We are taught that we are entitled to obtain great wealth and work at it at all costs. We store up our treasures in barns and aim for the golden years of retirement where we golf and vacation until we die. And then maybe, "When I retire, I will serve the Lord."

People of God, we have been duped. This is not the destiny and fullness of calling that Jesus saved us for. It's time we wrestle with the worldview we have been told is our entitled right to life.

The father of my translator on a trip to the Himalayas was martyred when my translator was a little boy. At that time, he vowed to the Lord that he would serve Him and preach the gospel for his whole life and is now doing just that. His life is not his own.

My friend, Dr. Alexandria Watkins, recently opened her practice in North Dallas, and there are times she has to close her new practice so she can take the gospel to the nations. Does it make sense for her business plan? Probably not, but she's storing up her treasures in Heaven. Her life is not her own.

My daughter, Emily, seeks every opportunity to minister the gospel to her patients and families at a hospital in Virginia. Could this cost her job and even potentially her license? Yes. Has she weighed the cost? Yes. Her life is not her own.

I met a man in Israel, Dr. Steven Khoury. He is an Arab believer taking the gospel to both the Jews and Muslims. The favor of the Lord is on him, and many are encountering the truth of Jesus. He had to get to a point where he said, "If I die, I die." His boldness and courage made us long for an impartation of the same passion and zeal for the gospel. His life is not his own.

I could share many more real-life examples of those who give their wealth, their businesses, and their time all to Jesus. And their lives will be written on the scrolls of Heaven for all of eternity. The joyous invitation before you and me is this: Will you let Him do the same with your life? Will you give Him permission?

Would you dare to forsake the American dream and all of your logical plans for your life, including your finances, and follow Jesus? Today, will you give Him your mustard seed of faith and give Him your yes? Will you trust Him to take you on the grandest adventure of a lifetime? There is so much more in store for you and me.

The Lord called my precious aunt to follow Him and go for many, many years. She refused. The timing wasn't good; there was more work to do at school, more money to make, and more things to accomplish. Finally, the Lord captured her heart, and she said, "Yes." She only had a few years to partner with Jesus before she died of cancer. If the Lord is calling you, and you don't understand what the next step is, that's OK because He does. He wants you to give Him your yes and your surrender. He will show you His plan as you follow Him!

Jesus looks at you and loves you and says to you today: Follow Me!

Listen to this worship song: "Follow Me" by Casting Crowns

## TESTIMONY
### Deaf Ears Opened

I recently traveled to East Africa on a medical mission trip. Our team rented a small school where the doctors, nurses, and pharmacists set up their clinic. My job was to sit under a tent outside and share the gospel and pray with people.

One day, a lady brought an 8-year-old girl to my tent. I shared the gospel, and the lady received Jesus. I noticed the little girl was not responding to my invitation. The lady told me the girl was born deaf and could not hear anything.

Suddenly, in my spirit, I sensed I should pray for her, and I told the lady I wanted to pray for Jesus to heal her. I told my translator that we have to have faith enough to move a mountain.

Then I prayed and commanded in Jesus' name for her ears to be opened. After the fifth time, she said she could hear something. The sixth time she could hear more, and the seventh time she was completely healed.

Her name is Lillian. For the first time, she heard her name and got a big smile on her face and was so grateful. I sensed from God that He did not want her to live deaf for the rest of her life but to walk in freedom and healing. I praise God for He is alive and actively working in the lives of people and setting them free. Lillian received Jesus as her Lord that day!

Safeeya

# It's Time to Contend!

*"Not that I have already obtained all this, or have already arrived at my goal, but I press on to take hold of that for which Christ Jesus took hold of me. Brothers and sisters, I do not consider myself yet to have taken hold of it. But one thing I do:* ***Forgetting what is behind and straining toward what is ahead, I press on toward the goal to win the prize for which God has called me heavenward in Christ Jesus.*** *All of us, then, who are mature should take such a view of things. And if on some point you think differently, that too God will make clear to you.* ***Only let us live up to what we have already attained****."*
*-Philippians 3:12-16, emphasis added*

*"He is the one we proclaim, admonishing and teaching everyone with all wisdom, so that we may present everyone fully mature in Christ.* ***To this end I strenuously contend with all the energy Christ so powerfully works in me."***
*-Colossians 1:28-29, emphasis added*

*"Dear friends, although I was very eager to write to you about the salvation we share, I felt compelled to write and* ***urge you to*** *contend for the faith that was once for all entrusted to God's holy people."*
*-Jude 1:3, emphasis added*

*"As for us, we have all of these great witnesses who encircle us like clouds. So we must let go of every wound that has pierced us and the sin we so*

*easily fall into. Then we will be able to run life's marathon race with passion and determination, for the path has been already marked out before us. We look away from the natural realm and we focus our attention and expectation onto Jesus who birthed faith within us and who leads us forward into faith's perfection. His example is this: Because his heart was focused on the joy of knowing that you would be his, he endured the agony of the cross and conquered its humiliation, and now sits exalted at the right hand of the throne of God! So consider carefully how Jesus faced such intense opposition from sinners who opposed their own souls, so that you won't become worn down and cave in under life's pressures."*
*-Hebrews 12:1-3, TPT*

No generation has been prepared for this time in history like our generation. We are being made ready to carry a mantle like no one before us. The great cloud of witnesses (also translated as "martyrs") is cheering us on to our finish line. Jesus is interceding for us. We may feel ill-equipped or unprepared, but the pulsating power of Christ in us speaks another word.

We are being trained in the secret place to contend for our faith and for the gospel. According to Strong's Concordance and Thayer's Greek Lexicon, the original meaning of the word "contend" means:

> "... to struggle, literally (to compete for a prize) ...
> "1) to enter a contest: contend in the gymnastic games
> "2) to contend with adversaries, fight
> "3) metaph. to contend, struggle, with difficulties and dangers
> "4) to endeavor with strenuous zeal, strive: to obtain something"

Over the last couple of years, the Bride of Christ had been shaken to the core. The foundation of many (whether built on sand or rock) was revealed. Our faith was shaken, and it was strengthened. We came to find out whose voice was the loudest counsel—the world or the Spirit of God.

We had to come to grips with whom we were living and whether we would be people of courage or fear. The shaking showed what we were truly made of. The enemy sidelined many in this last season, but I am watching an army emerge with focused faith, a deeper passion for Jesus, and a conviction to live for Christ no matter the cost. Although the Church ran and hid with the rest of culture in the pandemic lockdown, many are now saying with bone-deep conviction, "I will not do that again." There's a new resolve for many in the Bride of Christ today because of pandemic years.

My last trip to South Asia was life and vision-transforming for me and our team. Our translator's father was martyred, and he vowed to the Lord he would preach the gospel fearlessly, just like his father. That's contending. **His prize was always Jesus—he just had a new reality of the rules of the game as it pertained to his enemy.** That story really hit my spirit because I wondered if I would have the same response to my suffering. Would it put a deeper resolve in me to share the gospel, or would I sit in self-pity and ask the Lord, "Why?" I feel like seasons of suffering have prompted the latter question rather than the first conviction. I want my contending not to include self-pity, self-loathing, and self-preservation. It's time to shake free from the focus of self and get Jesus in our eye's sight. Can you see Jesus on the other side of the finish line cheering you on? No more bellybutton gazing—it's time to run! It's time to build! It's time to move with the fire of God!

> "We must make a commitment to the land we are in to bring the fire of God—to confront people with the reality of God's zeal and to prepare the way of the Lord to see that zeal consume the people." -James Maloney, "The Dancing Hand of God"[44]

> "The key to revival is whether or not we're going to venture out and discover the secrets to uprooting Satan's strongholds. Revival is launched from heaven but must find a landing pad in the hearts of man. It takes a

covenant of God's will with man's preparation to bring revival." -Mario Murillo

Women of God, we cannot carry revival and contend for the faith if we have not first been consumed with Jesus. You can't carry what you don't contain, nor can you contend for what you don't carry. It all begins with the utmost surrender to Jesus and His purposes. When we realize what He paid for—for our abundant life, healing, and righteousness—the only response is worship in surrender. Revival isn't contingent on our giftings—it's contingent on our surrender.

There are some of you who have wrongly disqualified yourselves based on personal inadequacies, history, or perceived lack of giftings. I was praying through this prayer and sensed the need to bring it to you so we can run unhindered from inaccurate self-perceptions and hang-ups. Pray this prayer with me!

1. "I break, shatter, cut-off, dissolve, and destroy the iniquity that says I am not special.
2. I break, shatter, cut-off, dissolve, and destroy the iniquity that says that I do not have the same standing as others.
3. I break, shatter, cut-off, dissolve, and destroy the iniquity that says that others are smarter than me.
4. I break, shatter, cut-off, dissolve, and destroy the iniquity that says others are better than me.
5. I break off, shatter, cut-off, dissolve, and destroy the iniquity that says that others know more than I do.
6. I break, shatter, cut-off, dissolve, and destroy the iniquity that says others are more important than I am.
7. I break, shatter, cut-off, dissolve, and destroy the iniquity that says I am not good at anything.
8. I break, shatter, cut-off, dissolve, and destroy the iniquity that says I will not speak or laugh in public.

9. I break, shatter, cut-off, dissolve, and destroy the iniquity that says no one cares about me.
10. I break, shatter, cut-off, dissolve, and destroy the iniquity that says I cannot be taught anything."

-Paul Cox, "Generational Prayers—2022 Edition"[45]

You have been chosen and called to bring Jesus to the world. He has given you your unique voice, experiences, giftings, and intimacy with Himself. No one can do what you have been called to do. Break free of the lies you have believed and be one who raises her hand to carry revival to this nation and the nations.

> "... God is raising up an army that will break every chain. He is on the move all over the world. ... If you are in a relationship with Christ, you are in His army. If your heart is stirred to put Jesus on display ... then you can be sure that He will put you on display. You can do great things for the sake of His Kingdom if you believe and are willing to step out and take the *risk* (which is another way I often spell faith)." -Robby Dawkins, "Do Greater Things"[46]

It's harvest time. Let's go!

Listen to this worship song: "Build Your Church" by Elevation Worship and Maverick City Music

# TESTIMONY
## Jesus Healed Me

I started having lower right abdominal pain, so my primary doctor ordered an ultrasound to figure out the cause. My husband attended the appointment and witnessed the technician measuring an opening in my abdomen. As the technician pushed on my abdomen to get a better measurement, the pain increased. The result of the ultrasound was a large hernia, and the only option was surgical repair.

Despite the upsetting news, I did my best to maintain a positive outlook and attended a spiritual luncheon with my family and friends. I had signed up for a mission trip in January 2023 and was concerned I would not have enough time to recover from surgery to attend. My friend and mission trip leader, Julie, encouraged me to see Dr. Watkins. The next day, Dr. Watkins ordered an MRI and administered IV treatment to help alleviate the pain. Then she prayed healing over me and, simultaneously, I prayed in agreement with Dr. Watkins, fully believing Jesus can heal, "Jesus, put your hands over the opening of the hernia and knit it together."

Jesus is alive, sitting on the throne, and still doing miracles. In my spirit, I was with Jesus. I did not see Him face-to-face but felt His presence in the room. I felt warmth in my body and a hand on my lower abdomen. Dr. Watkins finished praying, but in my spirit, I wanted to stay with Jesus—a moment of purity, beauty and peace. A divine place to be. It took me a few minutes to open my eyes and come back to reality.

I left Dr. Watkins' office smiling and completely pain free, thinking it was the result of the IV treatment. Four days later, the MRI report showed no evidence of a hernia, which is a miracle! Praise God, I have not experienced pain since Jesus healed me. It's a miraculous healing. Thank You, Jesus!

Salpi

# Radical Deviants

*"When they saw the courage of Peter and John and realized that they were unschooled, ordinary men, they were astonished and they took note that* ***these men had been with Jesus****. But since they could see the man who had been healed standing there with them, there was nothing they could say. So they ordered them to withdraw from the Sanhedrin and then conferred together. 'What are we going to do with these men?' they asked. 'Everyone living in Jerusalem knows they have performed a notable sign, and we cannot deny it. But to stop this thing from spreading any further among the people, we must warn them to speak no longer to anyone* ***in this name****.'*

*"Then they called them in again and commanded them not to speak or teach at all* ***in the name of Jesus****. But Peter and John replied, 'Which is right in God's eyes: to listen to you, or to him? You be the judges!* ***As for us, we cannot help speaking about what we have seen and heard.'***

*"After further threats they let them go. They could not decide how to punish them, because all the people were praising God for what had happened. For the man who was miraculously healed was over forty years old."*
*-Acts 4:13-22, emphasis added*

They wouldn't stop; they couldn't stop testifying of the wonder of Jesus! All because the blood of Jesus made a way for the impossible to become normative. The resurrection made a way for the Spirit to come and consume them. They were overtaken by the love of Christ and the boldness of the Holy Spirit. We can't keep quiet about the glorious power and life-transforming love of Jesus, especially when He finds a willing vessel to flow through. There was no way these two were going to stop talking! Their message and the miracles that followed went hand in hand with Peter and John. And the commission on Jesus' lips for their new identity, *"'you will be my witnesses (Acts 1:8),'"* became the force to be reckoned with—especially with the religious!

> "Does it not stir up our hearts, to go forth and help them, does it not make us long to leave our luxury, our exceeding abundant light, and go to them that sit in darkness?" -Amy Carmichael

If you take in the words of the song we close with today, it's packed full of New Covenant theology! It was never about our striving or our perfection or performance; it was always and only about the victorious blood of Jesus to make us righteous, holy, and bold for the sake of the gospel. Because He paid it all, we can give it all. Because He gave everything, we have everything to give for the sake of Christ.

> Peter and John were willing to lay down their fear of man for the cause of Christ.
>
> They were willing to be punished and imprisoned for the cause of Christ.
>
> They were willing to hold back nothing for the cause of Christ.
>
> They were willing to pray boldly for the cause of Christ.
>
> They were willing to stand against opposition for the cause of Christ.
>
> They would not stop speaking for the cause of Christ.

Where do you find yourself? What are you willing to lay down for the sake of the gospel? Why do we not have the same fervor as Peter and John? Where has it gone?

We used to be the top sending nation for missionaries all over the world. It's why our nation was born—the most redeeming gift a nation can carry. Read the current state of affairs through the eyes of a Laotian believer by the alias name Tobias Issara:

> "We live in a globalized world where Christians in the West are more resourced and informed than ever but care less and less about God's global mission to establish his reign among every people, tongue, tribe, and nation. … We're living in a post-missional West where secularism has invaded our faith and churches have lost that missional edge. We've become cultural Christians and are more concerned with national interests like Super Bowls, Sunday services, personal security, freedom of expression and status quo spirituality. We don't actually want to change the world for Jesus because we are comfortable with just being in it."

How did we lose the fervor and passion where we can't stop talking about what we have seen and heard?

Peter and John probably passed that crippled man for years as they went daily to the temple to pray. But one day, Heaven stopped Peter and John and invited them into a divine encounter where their message would intersect with the power of God. You and I have all had these moments with Jesus if not only at the moment of salvation. But there is more for us if we would only get to the place of love and boldness where we can't stop speaking about what we have seen and heard because we know the very God of the universe personally!

More than 3.4 billion people around the world are waiting for you, who have been with Jesus, transformed by His love, filled with His Spirit, and sent to the world. This invitation into a life of radical deviance from our post-missional West is for you!

> "We shall have all eternity to celebrate the victories, but we have only the few hours before sunset in which to win them." -Amy Carmichael

The Holy Spirit has impressed on me for Arise to emphasize a missionary movement by which we redeem this hour in our nation and raise up missionaries who will go and speak of what they have seen and heard. It will redeem the darkness that is rolling in over America. There are no age or demographical requirements, just those willing to raise their hands and say, "Yes," to His calling. Some women will be shifting vocations entirely, and some will be shifting priorities. But the Spirit of the Lord is raising up many in this hour who are willing to forsake the luxuries of life for the cause of Christ. The table of opportunity is large, and there is a seat for you.

Let me close with an excerpt from a fabulous book, "The Mind of a Missionary" by David Joannes. May it challenge you to raise your hand and say, "Yes," to a radically supernatural, Holy Spirit-led life.

> "Do you desire to thrive on mission as you make known the glory of God to those around you? Radical obedience to the commands of Christ calls for countercultural nonconformity. Do you want to see God's Kingdom established on the earth? Dive headfirst into the deep end of an unchartered adventure with your Heavenly Father. He will guide the water's current and lead you to places you never thought possible. Make no mistake, this manner of unreserved compliance to the King's commission is not the common course of action. Your friends may call you crazy; even your family members might turn their lip and question your motivations. Common sense compels you

to conform to the generally accepted, highly-overrated *modus operandi.* Don't give in. Status quo is not all it's cracked up to be. God values joyful acquiescence and willful obedience. He desires to journey with you and to show you the path of life. Only in His presence will you find fullness of joy and pleasures forevermore."[47]

It's time! Let's go!

Listen to this worship song: "The Blood" by Bethel Music, featuring Mitch Wong

# TESTIMONY
## Aneurism Gone

After adjusting his hearing aid, I asked my patient how I could pray for him. He looked at me confused, but I pressed in and said, "I'm going to pray for you. What do you need from God?" His face turned red, and he immediately started crying, pointing to his wife to speak for him. She said, "We just found out yesterday that he's been diagnosed with an aneurism, and the doctor got us in with a specialist tomorrow." I put my hands on his head where he directed, and his wife came over and put her hands on him, too. I declared, "Aneurism, be gone in Jesus' name. Clear report from the doctor." I hugged them, and they left. The next day he texted to tell me that the doctor said it was gone! Praise Jesus!

Heather

# Our First and Only Priority

*"'Anyone who **loves** their father or mother more than me is not worthy of me; anyone who **loves** their son or daughter **more than me** is not worthy of me. Whoever does not take up their cross and follow me is not worthy of me.'"*
*-Matthew 10:37-38, emphasis added*

*"Then Peter spoke up, 'We have left everything to follow you!' 'Truly I tell you,' Jesus replied, 'no one who has left home or brothers or sisters or mother or father or children or fields **for me and the gospel** will fail to receive a hundred times as much in this present age: homes, brothers, sisters, mothers, children and fields—along with persecutions—and in the age to come eternal life.'"*
*-Mark 10:28-30, emphasis added*

Our devotion to Jesus must be the highest and only priority in our lives as Christ followers.

> "The greatest danger of idolatry comes not from what is bad, but from what is *good*—like love in family relationships. The greatest danger to the *best* comes from *second best*." -David Guzik

Recently I boarded a flight to the mountains in South Asia where I would share the gospel with entire villages who had never heard the name of Jesus. I pondered and considered, "What if this costs me my very life?" It's not a fear of dying I consider but another level of being truly submitted and surrendered to Jesus in spite of any cost to me, my will, and even my family.

If Jesus truly has my heart, does He have permission and total access to rearrange my other and lesser affections to fall under His Lordship?

It grieves me to realize how so many believers in America (myself included) have succumbed to the great American dream and our entitlement to riches, comfort, retirement, and self-preservation. We have been duped and deceived because nowhere in Scripture do I see this lifestyle outlined for one who takes up her cross and follows Jesus. Nowhere in the world is this an ideology or worldview for our 70-80 years of living except in America. Our churches have boarded us upon cruise ships and preached grace at the cost of us having zero obligation to the Great Commission. We store up our wealth and wait for retirement and think, "Then, I will serve Jesus."

But what if God has another plan for us? What if He is asking you and me to lay down our retirement accounts, vacation time, sleep schedules, finances, business plans, time with our families and friends, free time, and vision for our lives and hand them over to Him? What if He wants to be the center of all of this to determine how it's spent? What if He asked you to give it all away for His sake? Would He even do such a thing? Yes.

We live in a paradox as a disciple of Jesus. We only find our lives when we lose them. And that only comes through dying—daily. Resurrection life comes after we pick up our cross, die to our will, and follow Jesus—daily. When criminals, sentenced to death in Jesus' days, picked up their crosses, they were meant for one thing: death. The cross has only ever meant one thing: death. But Jesus says we find life—true life—when we walk this road of ultimate surrender. And from this place of desperate endings, we walk in newness and the resurrection life of Christ. All things fall under His counsel, provision, and rulership. For human beings wanting to rule our lives, this is impossible unless Jesus becomes the center, and His love dictates our roads of faithfulness.

The gospel is offensive if we follow Jesus and His plan and His agenda and His purposes. This means we allow Him to be Lord over it all—everything that He has given us to love and steward. It all belongs to Him. Preachers across our nation have preached that Jesus should be first in your life, then your spouse, then your children, then ministry. But where is that in Scripture? To set up a neat little hierarchical structure of priorities is just another form of law, where we check the boxes on our performance and time management. It requires little faith, quite honestly, just a good perspective on our yearly planners.

If we really understand the reorganization of the life of Christ followers, we would see that Jesus is the center, and all things flow out of that. The Holy Spirit is one who determines, by His counsel, what we give our time, attention, affection, and resources to. It's like the illustration of a wheel, where Jesus is the hub, and every spoke that has been given to us is connected to the strongest part of the wheel, holding all things together. It moves in motion, and it takes ground, but Jesus is the center. If Jesus is just another spoke, and we sit in the middle of that wheel, it's no different than when the Hindus accept Christ to add Him as just another one of their gods. Church, we have to get this if we are going to be able to endure to the end. What will be required of your faith in the coming days, until Jesus returns, demands a reorganization of the mentality of following Jesus. There's just no way around it.

**An upside-down Kingdom, ruled by love, means an upside-down life centered in love, Himself.**

> "These people are called Christians. They hear the gospel, believe it, and are transformed by it. They are born again into an intimate love affair with the living God, and nothing can shake their confidence in Him. They are not bold in their own right or because they have tried hard. They are not the superstars of the Christian world. They are

simply those who believe. They are childlike. They hear the voice of God, submit to it, and as a result become a unique race of people. They are God's literal body on the earth, carrying out His revealed will wherever they go by the power of the Holy Spirit.

"They are in love, and it is obvious. It's the thing that motivates them. They are compelled by love. They are free from seeking their own desires. They live to see people set free into the same love affair they enjoy. Their joy is contagious. Their laughter sets people free from addiction and self-hate. They seek the lost. They go after the one. They pursue the most hopeless situations, because they know love never fails. They raise the dead. They cast out devils. They heal the sick. They speak with authority. They are set free from sin. It shows on their face, because they have forgotten what shame feels like. They radiate God's glory. They reflect His goodness. They demonstrate His kindness. They share their food with the poor. They give without sparing. They never lack. They are God's kids, and the world knows it." -Peter Louis, "Back to the Gospel"[48]

Let these ones arise! The world is waiting for you!

Listen to this worship song: "Give Me Jesus" by UPPERROOM

# TESTIMONY
## Safeeya's Healing

My name is Safeeya, and I am from a Muslim background. Until this miracle happened to me, I had never experienced a healing in my life. I am now a follower of Jesus, and I have read about Jesus' healing people in the Bible. I have often wondered if this could happen to me.

As I was packing and getting ready to take a mission trip to China, I lifted my suitcase and my left arm and shoulder suddenly started to badly hurt. The next day, the pain was greater, and my arm started to swell. I was concerned because the pain was excruciating. I couldn't sleep on my left side or carry anything. I was desperate and concerned that I might not be able to travel.

I went to the doctor and was told the muscle was strained and I would have to take steroids and pain medicine that could cause drowsiness, which would not work since I was planning to travel overseas. Desperate, I prayed and asked God for His power to heal my body.

The next Sunday at church, as the pastor gave the benediction prayer, he asked, "Is there anyone here who has hurt their left shoulder?" I opened my eyes and looked around. He was looking right at me. Then he said, "God wants to heal you right now." I answered, "Pastor, I receive it." After that day, my pain became less and less, the swelling went away, and I was completely healed and pain-free before my flight to China. I praise God and thank Him for His healing power and mercy in my life.

Safeeya

# Until He Comes

*"Then he turned to his disciples and said privately, 'Blessed are the eyes that see what you see. For I tell you that many prophets and kings wanted to see what you see but did not see it, and to hear what you hear but did not hear it.'" -Luke 10:23-24*

This Scripture is as real for us today as it was for Jesus, looking eye to eye with His disciples. This is a now word, as our generation is seeing God displayed in great measure and hearing the wonders of Him covering entire nations and people groups. The great cloud of witnesses cheering us on knows that what has been entrusted to us to both carry and endure is a calling and privilege and honor. All eyes are on the Church in this hour. Will we endure until the end? Will we stay the course and contend for what has been placed in our hands? We could be the generation to usher in the greatest revival history has ever seen!

*"My message and my preaching were not with wise and persuasive words, but with a demonstration of the Spirit's power, so that your faith might not rest on human wisdom, but on God's power." -1 Corinthians 2:4-5*

I led a team to Latin America, to a country that was decimated by COVID-19 lockdowns, food shortages, lack of medicine during the pandemic, government control, and a strong spiritual root of witchcraft. And we get the honor of carrying Jesus to those who are waiting for our feet, shod with the gospel of peace. I can think of no greater privilege. (Will you pray that we are shielded from the forces of darkness and bring many into the arms of Jesus?)

I have been convinced over the last year that the revival we have been praying and contending for, for decades and generations, is here on a global scale; but I am not seeing it here in America, sadly enough. Signs and wonders are accompanying the gospel and confirming our message. These are new days of great power and boldness for those who are entrusted with the gospel. I want to encourage you that God is moving beyond what we see and hear over social media and mainstream media outlets. He is drawing people to Himself at an accelerated rate! The clock is ticking.

Do you know your crystal clear calling in this hour? Do you have the conviction of your heart that will allow you stay the course and live in utter dependence on Christ in you?

People are waiting for you to open your mouth and declare the gospel. People are waiting for you to be willing to lose your life for the sake of them gaining eternal life.

People are waiting for us to get over being strapped down by distractions, doubt, intellectualism, fear, and excuses and show them the gospel of Christ.

*"He said to them, 'Go into all the world and preach the gospel to all creation. Whoever believes and is baptized will be saved, but whoever does not believe will be condemned. And these signs will accompany those who believe: In my name they will drive out demons; they will speak in new tongues; they will pick up snakes with their hands; and when they drink deadly poison, it will not hurt them at all; they will place their hands on sick people, and they will get well.'" -Mark 16:15-18*

I was speaking with a dear friend, Joy, who is 78 and has studied and taught the Bible for decades. She said to me with so much conviction, "We are in the final days of the Church age before the tribulation." We have been afforded time, beloved Church, but it's narrowing. The Great Commission is for us now! Preach the gospel, lay hands on the sick, and drive out demons. Your commission is not an option or menu item on a long list of Christian activities. Christ in you lived with this commission as He walked the Earth and now lives inside of millions of believers who have been **called** to this moment in history. We have a responsibility to the lost. They need to hear the good news and see with their own eyes the victorious power of Christ. He lives in you and has commissioned (sent) you with His *dunamis* power to make Him known throughout the Earth!

> *"So Paul and Barnabas spent considerable time there, speaking boldly for the Lord, who confirmed the message of his grace by enabling them to perform signs and wonders." -Acts 14:3*

By the grace of God, you open your mouth, and He will fill it. By the grace of God, you place your hands on the sick by faith, and He does the miracle. Your hands work in beautiful tandem to love the lost and show them the God who saves! The only thing that is contingent is your will to go and to speak and to pray. God will not force you in this hour to share hope with those who are perishing. You do have a will in the matter. Yet:

> *"How, then, can they call on the one they have not believed in? And how can they believe in the one of whom they have not heard? And how can they hear without someone preaching to them? And how can anyone preach unless they are sent? As it is written: 'How beautiful are the feet of those who bring good news!'" -Romans 10:14-15*

It's your beautiful feet He wants storming the gates of Hell to take back the lost. It's your feet He's anointed and positioned in areas of influence and opportunity that have been assigned to only you. Just like the blind beggar in Acts 3 who had been assigned to Peter and John, you have people assignments! What if you have someone waiting for you in a specific nation but you keep saying, "No," because your perceived timing or funding or fear or vacation time or life choices won't allow you to go? Ponder that for a moment.

*"After this the Lord appointed seventy-two others and sent them two by two ahead of him to every town and place where he was about to go. … 'Heal the sick who are there and tell them, "The kingdom of God has come near to you."'" -Luke 10:1, 9*

*"… because our gospel came to you not simply with words but also with power, with the Holy Spirit and deep conviction. You know how we lived among you for your sake." -1 Thessalonians 1:5*

The clock is ticking. It's go time! It's time to contend for this precious gospel and not let go in order to build our lives against the American dream and the fantasy of safety and self-preservation. The harvest is ripe, and people are waiting for **you**!

Listen to this worship song: "Revive Us Again" by Phil Wickham

## TESTIMONY
### Hearing Restored

My patient's wife wears a special hearing aid (CROS) designed for when one ear is normal and the other is "dead." She had been violently assaulted 25 years earlier, which caused hearing loss in her right ear. She told me she was ready to get a better CROS. I scheduled her for a retest but asked if I could pray for her before she left.

The next day I did a thorough case history, because of her multiple surgeries and medications, to ensure I didn't miss anything. When I finished her left ear and began testing her "dead" ear, I put the appropriate masking noise in her good ear to ensure an accurate test. I was bewildered to see her responding to the cue in an ear she shouldn't have been able to hear out of. I kept increasing the masking noise in her left ear, but she still heard the tone in her right ear, even at only 10 decibels. I checked my equipment multiple times and continued into each frequency with the same results. Suddenly it hit me! The only possible way she could hear out of her "dead" ear was that she'd been healed. I started crying and looked through the glass into the testing room where she was pointing to her right ear—and she was crying, too! When I finished her exam, she came out and hugged her husband, exclaiming, "I've been healed!" We celebrated, thanked Jesus together, and determined she did not need a hearing aid!

Heather

# The Word of the Lord Came to You—Go!

*"**The word of the Lord came to Jonah** son of Amittai: '**Go** to the great city of Nineveh and preach against it, because its wickedness has come up before me.'*

*"But Jonah ran away from the Lord and headed for Tarshish. He went down to Joppa, where he found a ship bound for that port. After paying the fare, he went aboard and sailed for Tarshish to flee from the Lord.*

*"**Then the Lord sent a great wind on the sea, and such a violent storm arose that the ship threatened to break up**. All the sailors were afraid and each cried out to his own god. And they threw the cargo into the sea to lighten the ship. But Jonah had gone below deck, where he lay down and fell into a deep sleep. The captain went to him and said, 'How can you sleep? Get up and call on your god! Maybe he will take notice of us so that we will not perish.' ...*

*"**At this the men greatly feared the Lord**, and they offered a sacrifice to the Lord and made vows to him. Now the Lord provided a huge fish to swallow Jonah, and Jonah was in the belly of the fish three days and three nights."*
*-Jonah 1:1-6, 16-17, emphasis added*

*"**One day Jesus said to his disciples,** "Let us **go** over to the other side of the lake." So they got into a boat and set out. As they sailed, he fell asleep.* ***A squall came down on the lake, so that the boat was being swamped, and they were in great danger****. The disciples went and woke him, saying, 'Master, Master, we're going to drown!'*

*"He got up and rebuked the wind and the raging waters; the storm subsided, and all was calm. 'Where is your faith?' he asked his disciples.* ***In fear and amazement*** *they asked one another, 'Who is this? He commands even the winds and the water, and they obey him.'"*
*-Luke 8:22-25, emphasis added*

Before the foundation of the world, the Lord had planned great exploits for both Jonah's and for Jesus' disciples. A city and a region both needed revival. He knew that if He could get His word to them, He could get it through them. Each of them had their moment to step into a divinely appointed time to bring an encounter to a king and a demon-possessed man.

Jonah wasn't super keen on his calling to Nineveh, and so he fled to the furthest, most opposite place from his assignment. The Lord called him east, but he went west! The Lord called him to travel to a city, but Jonah set sail on the sea to the end of the world as he knew it. But God is the God who sees and is familiar with all our ways, and there was a city that needed to be saved. Someone had to go.

Take a look at the disciples. Commanded to go, they jumped in a boat with Jesus, clearly directed as to where they were heading. All was good until the storm raged, and they lost sight of both their calling to go, their destination, and their reality that Jesus was with them. On the other side was a demon-possessed man who was crying out for help. God heard him. In fact, He didn't only hear him, but He also heard the whole region that was ready for an encounter with Jesus (Luke 8:38-39). Someone had to go.

I find these two passages beautifully parallel one another as they each had the word of the Lord to bring revival to a designated place. God clearly knew the outcome even when they couldn't see it in the middle of the storm, in the bottom of a boat, or in the belly of a fish. But He is faithful to fulfill His promises (Psalm 145:13), and He will do everything to keep us on track!

They were given a destination and a direction because God's mercy never relented for His people or for those far from Him. Someone had to go and share. We don't like the storms of life, but in both cases, a storm was used to reroute their journeys so they could fulfill God's plan and purposes. Sometimes, the storm redirects us to the place God originally intended, but we are off either 1 degree or 180 degrees on our compass.

They both had to rely on God to calm the storm—one through a spoken word and one through an offering. And in the midst of this reality, people saw God! In spite of their frailty and fear, both resulted in the salvation of many. A king and a demon-possessed man became the conduits of God's salvation and mercy to a city and a region. Anyone can be used by the Lord to bring revival!

> "Jonah could not see that deep within the terror of the storm God's mercy was at work, drawing him back to change his heart. It's not surprising that Jonah missed this initially. He did not know how God would come into the world to save us. We, however, living on this side of the cross, know that God can save through weakness, suffering, and apparent defeat. Those who watched Jesus dying saw nothing but loss and tragedy. Yet, at the heart of that darkness the divine mercy was powerfully at work, bringing about pardon and forgiveness for us. God's salvation came into the world through suffering, so his saving grace and power can work in our lives more and more as we go through difficulty and sorrow. There's mercy deep inside our storms." -Timothy Keller, "The Prodigal Prophet"[49]

Now it's our turn, dear sisters!

*"Then Jesus came to them and said, 'All authority in heaven and on earth has been given to me. Therefore* ***go*** *and make disciples of all nations, baptizing them in the name of the Father and of the Son and of the Holy Spirit, and teaching them to obey everything I have commanded you. And* ***surely I am with you always****, to the very end of the age.'"*
*-Matthew 28:18-20, emphasis added*

We have our destination and our direction—to take the gospel to the ends of the Earth! In this case, it's OK to get a one-way ticket to the end of the world! We have the Word of the Lord commanding us to open our mouths and speak because the compassion and mercy for lost people and nations reside in us in the person of Jesus! Some of you have been running from this command your whole life, and storm after storm, Jesus is trying to redirect you to your port of entry, where He is calling you to put your anchor down. God's command to go and tell was the same for Jonah as it was for Jesus' disciples and as it is for us today. Nothing has changed because God seeks to save the lost through our surrendered yes to Him—a life laid before Him no matter what the cost. Christ in us is compelled to run to a dying world. If we are headed in the wrong direction, it's time to reroute first our hearts toward Him and then our feet. Revival is not pending; it is here! What we have been praying for decades is now upon us, and a Bride who is awakened will be the one to harvest what God has prepared for her. I beseech you: do not dismiss your directive to co-mission with God in this hour! Don't spend three days in the metaphorical belly of a fish to get you to the place that He has been telling you to go. There's no time to waste, dear sisters. Many are in the valley of decision, and if we open our mouths, eternity will change for them.

As I've shared before, for years and years, the Lord had been calling my aunt to give up her teaching job and follow Him into a new season of ministry. For years she determined it wasn't time; she still had more to do. It was impractical. Maybe next year. Finally, she had a profound encounter with the Lord, resigned from her teaching job, and followed Jesus. She was able to partner with Jesus over the next few years before being diagnosed with pancreatic cancer which took her life. I always wonder about the fruit of what could have been if only she had said, "Yes," when He originally asked. It may not look practical to you, but if God is calling you to jump overboard head first, you better believe it will be the adventure of a lifetime, and He will provide everything you need. With all that I am, I implore you to run into your greatest commission with the God of the universe! There's nothing better! Cities, regions, and nations have been assigned to you! It's time to go!

> "Do you know where the hope for your city is? It's sitting in your chair right now. God's plan for revival for your city is you—Him working in and through you. There's no need to wait for something else to come. You've come. And because you've come, Christ has shown up. I pray that you believe that. I pray that you grab hold of God's promises for you. Christ came to seek and save what was lost and to destroy the works of the enemy. Because taking His power and presence to the streets is important to Him, it's got to be important to you and me." -Robby Dawkins, "Do What Jesus Did"[50]

Meet me in the harvest fields; they are ripe and ready! Let's go!

Listen to this worship song: "Promises" by Maverick City Music, featuring Joe L. Barnes and Naomi Raine

## TESTIMONY
### Children are a Heritage From the Lord

A few friends and I were invited to travel to South America to help cast vision on how to be intentional in activating healing and evangelism for new church plants. On Saturday during the training, as we gave more in-depth training, the Lord began to touch people's lives and bodies. We praised God for the 80 healings people testified to during that time.

On Sunday morning during the time of worship, as I was about to guide us in a healing service, the Holy Spirit gave me a vision. As I closed my eyes, I saw a black background with a white contrast of a tiny baby. I asked the Holy Spirit what this meant. I sensed His response in my spirit:

There is a woman here who is not able to get pregnant.

This was the first time I had received a vision related to praying for healing (a miracle), as healing prayers were new to me.

With the vision in mind, we entered into the healing activation time and, as the church prayed one for another, I instructed the people who were with this woman (not knowing who it was or if there was someone there unable to get pregnant) to pray for her with the simple biblical mandate that the Lord gave from the beginning of Scripture to *"'Be fruitful and multiply (Genesis 1:28, ESV).'"* I instructed them to speak that over her, and for her to say how many children she wanted to have. As we had discussed leading up to the activation time, the other two people in her group were to place their hands on her stomach and speak directly to the issue in faith.

After two weeks in the United States, I returned to South America and, within a few days, was informed by a woman that she was pregnant! She told me a little bit of her story about how she and her husband had a miscarriage and had not been able to get pregnant in this season. We rejoiced in the Lord and continue to be in awe of His majesty and supernatural power.

*"Children are a heritage from the Lord, offspring a reward from him. Like arrows in the hands of a warrior are children born in one's youth. Blessed is the man whose quiver is full of them. They will not be put to shame when they contend with their opponents in court." -Psalm 127:3-5*

Preston

# Do Not Limit What or Whom God Will Fill

*"Then the disciples went out and preached everywhere, and the Lord worked with them and confirmed his word by the signs that accompanied it." -Mark 16:20*

*"Everyone was filled with awe at the many wonders and signs performed by the apostles." -Acts 2:43*

*"'Now, Lord, consider their threats and enable your servants to speak your word with great boldness. Stretch out your hand to heal and perform signs and wonders through the name of your holy servant Jesus.'* ***After they prayed****, the place where they were meeting was shaken. And they were all* ***filled with the Holy Spirit and spoke the word of God boldly.****" -Acts 4:29-31, emphasis added*

*"Crowds gathered also from the towns around Jerusalem, bringing their sick and those tormented by impure spirits, and* ***all of them were healed****." -Acts 5:16, emphasis added*

*"Those who had been scattered preached the word* ***wherever they went****. ... When the crowds heard Philip and saw the signs he performed, they all paid close attention to what he said. For with*

*shrieks, impure spirits came out of many, and many who were paralyzed or lame were healed." -Acts 8:4, 6-7, emphasis added*

*"There he found a man named Aeneas, who was paralyzed and had been bedridden for eight years. 'Aeneas,' Peter said to him,* ***'Jesus Christ heals you****. Get up and roll up your mat.' Immediately Aeneas got up. All those who lived in Lydda and Sharon saw him and turned to the Lord." -Acts 9:33-35, emphasis added.*

*"So Paul and Barnabas spent considerable time there, speaking boldly for the Lord, who* ***confirmed the message of his grace by enabling them to perform signs and wonders.****" -Acts 14:3, emphasis added*

*"God did extraordinary miracles through Paul, so that even handkerchiefs and aprons that had touched him were taken to the sick, and their illnesses were cured and the evil spirits left them." -Acts 19:11-12*

**Healing, miracles, signs, and wonders are possible through Christ followers!**

Recently my friend went to get a massage. The night before, a man prophesied to her, "You have a double portion of anointing for the gift of healing." Before her massage therapist began, he complained of arthritic pain in his finger. About 10 minutes into the massage, he touched her right leg and felt a sharp pain through his finger. She felt her body and hands get very hot before this moment. He jumped back, quite startled, and the very words out of her mouth were, "The Lord just healed you." Sure enough, all of the pain in his finger was gone!

This is the life Jesus made possible! It testifies to His goodness and His wonder. Can you even imagine this baby church in Acts just beginning to walk, and there she goes, moving in signs, wonders, and miracles? All of it testified, pointed to, and gave glory to Jesus! All of this gave context to the finished work of the cross. Many were saved because they could see the miracles with their very eyes. Somehow, we have settled for a powerless gospel, as long as we have truth. The truth of the matter is that these wonders and miracles draw us deeply into the heart of Father, Jesus, and Holy Spirit. He goes out of His way to display wonder upon wonder (Isaiah 29:14)!

For a harvest to take place, you better believe it takes a demonstration and proclamation of the gospel! They go hand in hand for us just like they did for Paul, Peter, and the early church. People need to see with their eyes, hear with their ears, and perceive with their spirits the depth of the goodness of God. Jesus can work through us to accompany our preaching with signs and wonders.

**We have the privilege of putting the power of Jesus on display!**

When Jesus commissioned us to go and make disciples of all nations, it was not because He wanted us to have a routine life of boring religion! He wanted us to live the greatest adventure of a lifetime—faith accompanied with the power of the Spirit, flowing out of our lives like a gushing river!

> "When we live in the river of God, totally immersed in His heart, healing is released through us. Rich life springs up along the banks and shores of our lives. Pure water from God transforms and purifies any other murky waters we may face. It makes salty or bitter waters fresh." -Heidi Baker, "Birthing the Miraculous"[51]

**Boldness in preaching the gospel or praying for the sick is a gift from God to release the Kingdom of Heaven here on Earth.**

It is possible for believers to move in this power and pray for this power. The early Christians prayed that God would send signs and wonders, and He answered them. This is our glorious partnership with Father, Jesus, and Holy Spirit! Even as persecution ensued for the early church, these sudden missionaries were sent out, and their very lives released the Kingdom. The phrase *"wherever they went (Acts 8:4)"* indicates they weren't hiding inside the four walls of their churches, hoping the lost would come to them. The persecution that was ensuing was sending them forth, and the Church was growing.

According to my missionary friends, Roland and Shirin, missiologists are identifying Iran's Christians as the fastest-growing church in the world. In fact, Iranian believers are now leading Afghan refugees to the Lord in the hundreds. (If you have never watched "Sheep Among Wolves Part Two", it will stir your heart in expectation!) Persecution is shaking the walls of the Christian Church just like it did in Acts 4, but the gospel is not being held back and stifled because of our unwillingness to go. Sometimes, He just has to shake the nest and get us to move! More than 3.4 billion people who have never heard the gospel need us to move!

> "In every church where there is really the power of the Spirit of God, the Lord will cause it to be spread abroad, more or less. He never means that a church should be like a nut shut up in a shell, nor like ointment enclosed in a box. The precious perfume of the gospel must be poured forth to sweeten the air." Charles Haddon Spurgeon, "All of It"[52]

**Do not limit what or whom God will fill as a conduit of His power and grace.**

Whether it be the robe of Jesus, the shadow of Peter, the handkerchief of Paul, or the very rocks crying out in the Earth, God will use anything and everything to bring Himself glory. He's not a respecter of people or position. He merely wants the gift of our faith and our worship. When my friend was getting a massage, she never said, "Be healed in the name of Jesus." She just laid there, and the power of God came to heal. There will be times we are urged by the Spirit to walk up to a stranger to pray for healing because the Lord is continually training us in faithful partnership and obedience. And at other times our presence in a place may release the presence of God to heal or bring the miraculous. Let's just get to the point where we don't resist Him with our limited perspective and unbelief. When He decides to act, He's the God of the impossible!

There are some of you reading this right now who struggle with unbelief. I want to pray for you. There are others reading this right now who have never had Jesus move through your lives like this. I want to pray for you. And for those longing for the gift of healing, I want to pray for you.

> Lord Jesus, I ask You to come and fall on my sisters who identify with one (or all) of these three categories. Would You fall with the anointing of faith to believe that You are the same God that we have read about in Scripture? Would You remove unbelief, fear, skepticism, and doubt? I ask that You would so move in the hearts, minds, and spirits of these women that You completely turn their worlds upside down. Lord, I ask You to give the gift of faith and the gift of healing. I pray for courageous boldness to rest on these women, that they would release the Kingdom of God in power and faith, bringing You all the glory! You are no respecter of people, so do what You long to do through their surrendered lives, in the name of Jesus!

Listen to this worship song: "Too Good to Not Believe" by Cody Carnes

# TESTIMONY

## Healing of a Buddhist High Priest in the Name of Jesus

In the middle of our hardest and longest day of hiking, I came to the most ornate Buddhist temple I had seen in that area. I felt a check in my spirit to not step onto the property of the temple when God brought the high priest of the temple from around the corner who invited us to his home. We sat with the man, his 89-year-old mother, his brothers, and temple workers. My translator maintained conversation with him while he was giddy to have an English speaker at his home. With best efforts, he would say little phrases in English to try and communicate with me. Eventually, my translator instructed me to share the gospel with this man in English, without translation, just to have it shared. This didn't seem like the best setup for him to understand truth, but I began to share with the leading of the Holy Spirit.

He was tuned into every word I said whether his mind understood it fully. When I finished sharing the story of Jesus, I asked if he wanted to receive the free gift being offered to him. He gave one of the typical responses for people of his faith background, that he believed it was good news, but he wasn't willing to give up his cultural beliefs.

My translator continued conversation with him while I sat to the side having my own dialogue with the Lord. I knew he heard the Kingdom of God proclaimed. Now it was time for the Kingdom of God to be demonstrated for him and his household. I asked the Holy Spirit to give me a word of knowledge to get the attention of this man who is meant to be a redeemed child of God. I saw in my mind the word "accident" and the number "9." When I found a break in their conversation, I interjected, asking if I could ask a question. As I presented the question of whether he possibly had an accident when he was 9 years old, he sat back a little astonished in recalling the fact that the accident that severed parts of his finger indeed happened when he was 9 years old. I followed up with the truth that there is no way that I, in myself, could have known this fact, but

God sees him and knows every detail about his life. Believing and having seen the healing power of God through praying in the name of Jesus, I asked if I could lay my hands on his finger to pray for healing.

In a simple prayer to tell pain to go and for healing to come in the name of Jesus, he exclaimed through a smile that he felt a refreshing cool peace come over his body. I asked if the pain was going away when he explained that pain hadn't been an issue since the nerves were damaged. Therefore, I changed my wording to speak life and restoration back into his nerve endings. He almost jumped out of his chair as he moved his finger with more ease than he had since he was a child. He began to feel sensations and movements because of the loving kindness of Jesus bringing healing to what was once broken.

The evidence of this man being a person of peace was showcased in his next move. He immediately called his family and workers back to where we were standing for them to also receive prayer in the name of Jesus. His mother first explained the pain in her knees and lack of movement from a poor surgery done to her wrist years ago. Jesus quickly healed her knee pain, and she bounced up and down like a child with newfound joy.

One of the farmers at the temple came up with a face expressing the amount of pain he was in. I laid my hands on his lower back and simply spoke to his body and the injury to be healed in the name of Jesus and stepped away to see if there was still pain. He sat up, cracked his neck from one side, then the other, and while remaining speechless he walked away upright with shock in his eyes about what he was experiencing.

My translator and I felt the peace that our work there was done. We had shared the good news of Jesus, and these people witnessed the hand of God move in mighty ways. We walked away believing for and praying that the seeds that had been planted would continue to be watered. The possibility of the high priest of that temple on a populated mountain coming to claim Jesus as his King could be a mighty advance for the Kingdom of Heaven due to the influence that one man has on the people in surrounding villages.

Hannah

## DAY 40

# The Commission

*"Blessed is the one who reads aloud the words of this prophecy, and blessed are those who hear it and take to heart what is written in it, because the time is near." -Revelation 1:3*

*"'Look, I am coming soon! Blessed is the one who keeps the words of the prophecy written in this scroll.'" -Revelation 22:7*

When I was just 6 years old, my mom sat my brother and me down on our long, yellow, corduroy sofa. I remember my feet didn't even hang over the edge of the cushions. She shared with us that she had just finished a book on the return of Jesus, and the Lord impressed on her that He was coming back, and she was not ready. She gave her life fully to Jesus and shared the gospel with me and my brother. I remember hearing her words about Jesus and salvation through Him and knowing in my heart and mind that what she was sharing was absolute truth. My brother (4) and I both gave our lives to Jesus that day. Our whole family was saved, and six years later my parents sold everything and moved us to Germany to be missionaries so they could take the gospel behind the Iron Curtain. I share this story of my salvation all over the world. I am so thankful that my mom spared me from a life without Christ. Praise God for our moms (and dads) who tell us about Jesus when we are young so we can avoid life without Him! I just love my mom!

My family and I went on a lovely vacation recently. It was to celebrate me having turned 50 in March. I would wake up each morning to spend time with Jesus as He had me eagerly devouring the book of Revelation. Having spent some time building a solid foundation of understanding the rapture and tribulation, I read this book with a whole new perspective. For the first time, it made so much sense. I never understood where I existed in that book—what was mine and what wasn't mine. Where did I fit in the timeline of the seals, trumpets, and bowl judgements? The answer is nowhere. That isn't for me. It isn't for anyone who is in Christ Jesus. Walking into this book with a deeper understanding had me read with a sober mindfulness of what is soon approaching for those who are not in Christ. The wrath of God outlined from Chapter 6 is about what will take place during the seven years of tribulation, the Second Coming, millennial reign of Christ, and the final battle. What is ours to work through with the Holy Spirit is chapters 1-3 (until we return back on the scene in Chapter 19). Do any of those warnings apply to you or me in our current walk with Jesus? That's one thing we need to take before the Lord.

Jesus says, *"'Look, I am coming soon (Revelation 22:7)!'"* Another translation for "soon" is "suddenly." He will come like a thief in the night when we are not expecting His return. Is your lamp filled with oil? Are you ready for His sudden and imminent return? My mom was not that day back in 1979, and in an instant, our whole family was saved. She did not hold this truth to herself but from that time forward, lived to tell everyone about Jesus.

*"'Blessed is the one who keeps the words of the prophesy written in this scroll (Revelation 22:7).'"* How do we keep these words? According to Strong's Exhaustive Concordance, to keep means to attend to carefully, to take care of, to guard, to keep one in the state in which he is, to observe, to reserve, and to undergo something.

How do we attend to these prophecies that literally caused John to feel sick when he saw them. He was undone by what God showed him is coming on a world that has rejected Christ. We are to hide these things in our hearts, almost like Mary did in her observation of the first coming of Jesus. It is time we take them to heart, to see what John saw that is coming upon the world very soon. Many believe that we as believers in Jesus will not be here to observe them—we will be with Jesus during that time. But for those you love who are far from Christ, this will be their reality. Oh, God, let us be undone by that sober truth.

> "God has given us 2,000+ years to prepare for the coming storm that will sweep the entire earth. When that happens, there will be no place to hide. Plagues, earthquakes, hail, fire, and starvation will run rampant throughout the whole globe. COVID will seem like a case of the sniffles in comparison to what people will be exposed to during the seven-year global catastrophe. 'Blessed' almost feels like an understatement for those will escape this time." -Amir Tsarfati, "Revealing Revelation"[53]

Therefore, I must ask the question: How does the book of Revelation shape our urgency of sharing the gospel with the lost?

We can't just read the words of this letter without taking them to heart. (Well, I guess we can!) Oh, Lord, transform us by Your Word! Revelation is a prophetic warning of what is soon approaching as the world stage is being quickly set for a one-world government, currency, religion, and leader. But Jesus is our conquering King who reigns in victory! He has salvation in store for those who desire Him. He has given us the playbook for the end of days and His victory over Satan. We know the story, and if we keep it to ourselves, what good is that for those who are perishing?

*"How, then, can they call on the one they have not believed in? And how can they believe in the one of whom they have not heard? And how can they hear without someone preaching to them? And how can anyone preach unless they are sent? As it is written: 'How beautiful are the feet of those who bring good news!'" -Romans 10:14-15*

What is profound is the blessing that comes with reading this book and allowing it to shape and change us. The book of Revelation is packed full of blessings—seven final blessings that we read in this last love letter. It comes with great warning and great reward if we hear and apply what God is saying:

*"Blessed is the one who reads aloud the words of this prophecy, and blessed are those who hear it and take to heart what is written in it, because the time is near." -Revelation 1:3*

*"Then I heard a voice from heaven say, 'Write this: Blessed are the dead who die in the Lord from now on.' "Yes,' says the Spirit, 'they will rest from their labor, for their deeds will follow them.'" -Revelation 14:13*

*"'Look, I come like a thief! Blessed is the one who stays awake and remains clothed, so as not to go naked and be shamefully exposed.'" -Revelation 16:15*

*"Then the angel said to me, 'Write this: Blessed are those who are invited to the wedding supper of the Lamb!' And he added, 'These are the true words of God.'" -Revelation 19:9*

*"Blessed and holy are those who share in the first resurrection. The second death has no power over them, but they will be priests of God and of Christ and will reign with him for a thousand years." -Revelation 20:6*

*"'Look, I am coming soon! Blessed is the one who keeps the words of the prophecy written in this scroll.'" -Revelation 22:7*

*"Blessed are those who wash their robes, that they may have the right to the tree of life and may go through the gates into the city.'" -Revelation 22:14*

Beloved, go tell the world about Jesus! Don't keep Him to yourself in the privacy of your life. Go with boldness and conviction that Jesus is the only way. If we would live with the imminent return of Christ ever before us, I believe it would be easy to count our lives as nothing. We are out of here, but those we love who don't know Him will endure more than we could even imagine. We must trust in His mercy on His people. But for those of you stuck in fear, shake it off. Ask the Lord to untie you and set you free to boldly proclaim the love and power of Jesus. It's time. We must go.

> "Jesus is coming, and He is bringing His reward with Him. What is that reward? It is to go to the place that He has prepared for us, and there to experience the *bema* seat judgement, during which we will be recompensed for our faithful service here on earth. Remember, He is not coming to take us to a judgement seat of salvation. That's not necessary, because if you are not a believer in Christ, you will not be going with Him. When we lift off from this earth, there is nothing but good waiting for us for the rest of eternity." -Amir Tsarfati, "Revealing Revelation"[54]

*"He who testifies to these things says, 'Yes, I am coming soon.' Amen. Come, Lord Jesus. The grace of the Lord Jesus be with God's people. Amen." -Revelation 22:20-21*

Listen to this worship song: "The Commission" by Cain

# About the Author

Julie King has been married to Michael for more than 26 years. They have had the privilege of watching their four daughters—Elizabeth, Emily, AnnMarie, and Grace—grow and develop a passion for Jesus and have a heart for the nations. Her family is the delight of her life.

Julie grew up as a missionary kid to parents who served on staff with Cru for 33 years. Much of her youth was spent living overseas in Germany, during the fall of the Berlin Wall and the opening of the Iron Curtain. It was a formative period for both her worldview and passion for the gospel. Today, Julie leads women around the world to take the gospel to people who have never heard the name of Jesus.

As an adult, Julie's desire and passion for the Bride of Christ and the lost—those who don't know Jesus personally—compelled her to begin a neighborhood Bible study to engage others in the Word and on mission. One result of this initiative was a prayer and worship gathering in Frisco, Texas, called God of the City: The Church unified-revived-unleashed. This three-year planting of the Lord was a movement to unite the church in North Dallas for the purpose of worship and prayer for revival. Hundreds of churches participated in the event, which was attended by thousands of people.

In 2018, Julie began an initiative called Arise through the mission of East-West. Through this effort, she is seeing women grow in a depth of hunger and passion for Jesus and His heart for the world. Julie serves as a full-time missionary with East-West.

Julie has a passion for the Word and for worship and loves rallying people to the very things God brings forth in her spirit. This book is a result of those passions, and she believes there's more to come.

# About East-West

East-West began because two men couldn't resist the call of Christ's great mission: go into the world and make disciples (Matthew 28:18-20).

Through their work behind the Iron Curtain in the early 1980s, East-West founders, John Maisel and Bud Toole, recognized the profound need to train church planters and pastors in nations with severely restricted Christian activity.

In May 1993, East-West was established to train and mentor faithful and reliable national pastors to become catalysts for indigenous church growth—reaching the lost with the gospel, equipping new believers, and multiplying reproducible churches.

Today, East-West works primarily in limited access countries and among unreached people groups in more than 40 countries worldwide so that disciples and churches will continuously multiply.

## VISION

The vision of East-West is to glorify God by multiplying followers of Jesus in the spiritually darkest areas of the world.

## MISSION

The mission of East-West is to mobilize the Body of Christ to evangelize the lost and equip local believers to multiply disciples and churches among the unreached.

## GET INVOLVED

To learn more about East-West or to join the global ministry, visit www.eastwest.org/get-involved.

# About Arise

Arise is an initiative born out of East-West's desire to empower women around the world to be used by God to take the gospel to the nations. This is done by calling, connecting, and commissioning them to one another and to the heart and purposes of God in this hour.

There is a call from the Lord for women right now to live in the authority and identity given to them by Christ. We are connecting women to each other through stories and experiences. And women are being commissioned to be a powerful force for the Kingdom of God.

That's why Arise exists.

We have hopeful expectation that as we call women to live boldly in the power of the Holy Spirit, connect them to each other for ongoing encouragement, and send them out on their unique mission, a culture of revival will break loose as families, communities, and nations are changed forever for the glory of God.

Why? Because it's happened in the past.

Through women of our ancient past (such as Deborah, Ruth, Mary, and Lydia) and women of recent centuries (including Joan of Arc, Amy Carmichael, Corrie ten Boom, Mother Teresa, and Heidi Baker), God changed the world.

We believe that women who are moved by a passionate love for Jesus and who partner with Him to build His Kingdom are key to unlocking gospel movements in the world's spiritually dark places.

And now we are believing God for 70 cities nationally and internationally to build this Kingdom movement and mobilize women.

To learn more or to get involved with Arise, visit www.eastwest.org/arise.

## Get Involved

It's time to discover your role in the Great Commission. Consider the following ways you can partner with East-West in God's Kingdom work.

**PRAY:** Prayer moves the mission. God works when we pray, which is why East-West is committed to passionate, consistent prayer for the unreached and our missionaries and national partners who serve among them. Prayer is our most powerful weapon against the kingdom of darkness; therefore, it is the greatest gift you can give to our ministry. You can join us in the important work of praying for those living in the throes of spiritual darkness as we seek to reach them with the good news of Jesus in a way that transforms their lives forever. Learn more about how you can partner with us in prayer at **www.eastwest.org/pray.**

**GIVE:** Your gift to East-West has eternal value. It continually expands our reach and multiples our impact as we seek to take the gospel to the lost. Each gift is an investment to reach the darkest areas of the world with the light of God's Word. With East-West, you are not investing in a fleeting kingdom of man but in an eternal Kingdom that cannot be shaken. You can give to the general ministry of East-West, to a missionary, to a region, or to a short-term mission team member. You can give now at **www.eastwest.org/give.**

**GO:** Join the movement of the gospel throughout the nations by partnering with East-West on the field. Because the Great Commission is for every believer, we're committed to empowering the global Church to reach the unreached. Through short-term teams, missionary deployments, and mid-term opportunities, we train and send people just like you to take the gospel where it's never been. As believers go, we are witnessing God's Kingdom invade the spiritually darkest areas of the world. Explore the different ways you can go with East-West at **www.eastwest.org/go.**

# Notes


1. Chan, Francis. *Letters to the Church.* (Colorado Springs: David C. Cook, 2018)
2. Metaxas, Eric. *Letter to the American Church.* (Washington: Salem Books, 2022)
3. Pierce, Mary Jo. *Follow Me: An Unending Conversation with Jesus.* (Southlake: Gateway Press, 2018)
4. Dawkins, Robby. *Do What Jesus Did: A Real-Life Field Guide to Healing the Sick, Routing Demons and Changing Lives Forever.* (Minneapolis: Chosen Books, 2013)
5. Guzik, David. *First and Second Thessalonians: Verse by Verse Commentary.* (Santa Barbara: Enduring Word Media, 2013)
6. Miskov, Jennifer, Clark, Randy, Engle, Lou. *Fasting for Fire: Igniting Fresh Hunger to Feast upon God.* (Shippensburg: Destiny Image Publishers: 2022)
7. Dawkins, Robby. *Do What Jesus Did: A Real-Life Field Guide to Healing the Sick, Routing Demons and Changing Lives Forever.* (Minneapolis: Chosen Books, 2013)
8. Rustenbach, Rusty. *A Guide for Listening and Inner-Healing Prayer: Meeting God in the Broken Places.* (Colorado Springs: Nav Press, 2011)
9. Guyon, Jeanne. *Experiencing the Depths of Jesus Christ: Library of Spiritual Classics, Volume 2.* (Sargent: SeedSowers Christian Books Publishing House, 1999)
10. King, Patricia. *A Prophetic Manifesto for the New Era: 20 Prophetic Words for the 2020s.* (Shippensburg: Destiny Image Publishers, 2020)
11. Zodhiates, Spiros. *The Hebrew Greek Key Word Study Bible: NASB-77 Edition.* (Chattanooga: AMG Publishers, 2008)
12. King, Patricia. *A Prophetic Manifesto for the New Era: 20 Prophetic Words for the 2020s.* (Shippensburg: Destiny Image Publishers, 2020)
13. Vallotton, Kris, Johnson, Bill. *The Supernatural Ways of Royalty: Discovering Your Rights and Privileges of Being a Son or Daughter of God.* (Shippensburg: Destiny Image Publishers, 2007)
14. Vallotton, Kris, Johnson, Bill. *The Supernatural Ways of Royalty: Discovering Your Rights and Privileges of Being a Son or Daughter of God.* (Shippensburg: Destiny Image Publishers, 2007)
15. Guzik, David. *Isaiah: Verse by Verse Commentary.* (Goleta: Enduring Word, 2021)

16. Johnson, Christy. *Releasing Prophetic Solutions: Praying Heaven's Promises over Your Home, Family, and Nation.* (Shippensburg: Destiny Image Publishers, 2020)
17. Guzik, David. *Mark: Verse by Verse Commentary.* (Goleta; Enduring Word, 2005)
18. Guzik, David. *Mark: Verse by Verse Commentary.* (Goleta; Enduring Word, 2005)
19. Dawkins, Robby. *Do What Jesus Did: A Real-Life Field Guide to Healing the Sick, Routing Demons and Changing Lives Forever.* (Minneapolis: Chosen Books, 2013)
20. Chan, Francis. *Forgotten God: Reversing Our Tragic Neglect of the Holy Spirit.* (Colorado Springs: David C. Cook, 2019)
21. Randall, Bill. *The Life Jesus Made Possible: Embracing the Kingdom Within our Reach.* (Long Wake: 2018)
22. Maloney, James. *The Dancing Hand of God Volume 1: Unveiling the Fullness of God Through Apostolic Signs, Wonders, and Miracles.* (Bloomington: WestBow Press, 2011)
23. Bolsinger, Tod. *Canoeing the Mountains: Christian Leadership in Uncharted Territory.* (Brentwood: InterVarsity Press, 2015)
24. Cox, Paul l, Cox, Brian P., Parker, Barbara Kain. *Generational Prayers: 2022 Edition.* (Apple Valley: Aslan's Place, 2022)
25. Murillo, Mario. *Vessels of Fire and Glory.* (Shippensburg: Destiny Image Publishers, Inc., 2020)
26. Platt, David. *Something Needs to Change: An Urgent Call to Make Your Life Count.* (Colorado Springs: Multnomah, 2019)
27. Green, Jessi. *Wildfires: Revolt Against Apathy and Ignite Your World with God's Power.* (Shippensburg: Destiny Image Publishers, Inc., 2021)
28. Aaron, Wade. *The Reward of the Lamb: A Journey of Discovering How to Walk Like Jesus.* (Warsaw: Tall Pine Books, 2021)
29. Aaron, Wade. *The Reward of the Lamb: A Journey of Discovering How to Walk Like Jesus.* (Warsaw: Tall Pine Books, 2021)
30. Kraft, Charles H. Defeating Dark Angels: *Breaking Demonic Oppression in the Believer's Life.* (Bloomington: Chosen Books, 2016)
31. Scazzero, Peter. *Emotionally Healthy Spirituality: It's Impossible to Be Spiritually Mature, While Remaining Emotionally Immature.* (Grand Rapids: Zondervan, 2017)
32. Bolz, Shawn. Encounter: *A Spiritual Perspective That Will Shape Your Faith for the Coming Move of God.* (Lake Mary: Charisma House, 2022)
33. King, Patricia. *A Prophetic Manifesto for the New Era: 20 Prophetic Words for the 2020s.* (Shippensburg: Destiny Image Publishers, 2020)

34. Ortlund, Dane C. Gentle and Lowly: *The Heart of Christ for Sinners and Sufferers.* (Wheaton: Crossway, 2020)
35. Ortlund, Dane C. Gentle and Lowly: *The Heart of Christ for Sinners and Sufferers.* (Wheaton: Crossway, 2020)
36. Louis, Peter. *Back to the Gospel: Reviving the Church through the Message that Birthed it.* (Dallas: Braveheart Ministries, Inc, 2017)
37. Joannes, David. *The Mind of a Missionary: What Global Kingdom Workers Tell Us About Thriving on Mission Today.* (Prescott: Within Reach Global, Inc. 2018)
38. Joannes, David. *The Mind of a Missionary: What Global Kingdom Workers Tell Us About Thriving on Mission Today.* (Prescott: Within Reach Global, Inc. 2018)
39. Joannes, David. *The Mind of a Missionary: What Global Kingdom Workers Tell Us About Thriving on Mission Today.* (Prescott: Within Reach Global, Inc. 2018)
40. Schlink, Basilea. *My All for Him: Fall in Love with Jesus All over Again.* (Bethany House Pub, 2000)
41. Joannes, David. *Gospel Privilege.* (Within Reach Global Inc. 2021)
42. Guzik, David. *James & 1-2 Peter: Verse by Verse Commentary.* (Goleta: Enduring Word Media, 2009)
43. Johnson, Bill. *God is Good: He's Better Than You Think.* (Shippensburg: Destiny Image Publishers, Inc., 2018)
44. Maloney, James. *The Dancing Hand of God Volume 1: Unveiling the Fullness of God Through Apostolic Signs, Wonders, and Miracles.* (Bloomington: WestBow Press, 2011)
45. Cox, Paul l, Cox, Brian P., Parker, Barbara Kain. *Generational Prayers: 2022 Edition.* (Apple Valley: Aslan's Place, 2022)
46. Dawkins, Robby. *Do Greater Things: Activating the Kingdom to Heal the Sick and Love the Lost.* (Bloomington, Chosen Books, 2018)
47. Joannes, David. *The Mind of a Missionary: What Global Kingdom Workers Tell Us About Thriving on Mission Today.* (Prescott: Within Reach Global, Inc. 2018)
48. Louis, Peter. *Back to the Gospel: Reviving the Church through the Message that Birthed it.* (Dallas: Braveheart Ministries, Inc, 2017)
49. Keller, Timothy. *The Prodigal Prophet: Jonah and the Mystery of God's Mercy.* (New York: Viking, 2018)
50. Dawkins, Robby. *Do What Jesus Did: A Real-Life Field Guide to Healing the Sick, Routing Demons and Changing Lives Forever.* (Minneapolis: Chosen Books, 2013)
51. Baker, Heidi. *Birthing the Miraculous.* (Lake Mary: Charisma House, 2014)
52. https://www.spurgeon.org/resource-library/sermons/all-at-it/#flipbook/ Accessed 05/08/2023.

53. Tsarfati, Amir, Yohn, Rick. *Revealing Revelation: How God's Plans for the Future can Change your Life Now.* (Eugene: Harvest House Publishers, 2022)
54. Tsarfati, Amir, Yohn, Rick. *Revealing Revelation: How God's Plans for the Future can Change your Life Now.* (Eugene: Harvest House Publishers, 2022)

# Works Cited

1. Aaron, Wade. *The Reward of the Lamb: A Journey of Discovering How to Walk Like Jesus.* (Warsaw: Tall Pine Books, 2021)
2. Baker, Heidi. *Birthing the Miraculous.* (Lake Mary: Charisma House, 2014)
3. Bolsinger, Tod. *Canoeing the Mountains: Christian Leadership in Uncharted Territory.* (Brentwood: InterVarsity Press, 2015)
4. Bolz, Shawn. Encounter: *A Spiritual Perspective That Will Shape Your Faith for the Coming Move of God.* (Lake Mary: Charisma House, 2022)
5. Chan, Francis. *Forgotten God: Reversing Our Tragic Neglect of the Holy Spirit.* (Colorado Springs: David C. Cook, 2019)
6. Chan, Francis. *Letters to the Church.* (Colorado Springs: David C. Cook, 2018)
7. Cox, Paul l, Cox, Brian P., Parker, Barbara Kain. *Generational Prayers: 2022 Edition.* (Apple Valley: Aslan's Place, 2022)
8. Dawkins, Robby. *Do Greater Things: Activating the Kingdom to Heal the Sick and Love the Lost.* (Bloomington, Chosen Books, 2018)
9. Dawkins, Robby. *Do What Jesus Did: A Real-Life Field Guide to Healing the Sick, Routing Demons and Changing Lives Forever.* (Minneapolis: Chosen Books, 2013)
10. Green, Jessi. *Wildfires: Revolt Against Apathy and Ignite Your World with God's Power.* (Shippensburg: Destiny Image Publishers, Inc., 2021)
11. Guyon, Jeanne. *Experiencing the Depths of Jesus Christ: Library of Spiritual Classics, Volume 2.* (Sargent: SeedSowers Christian Books Publishing House, 1999)
12. Guzik, David. *First and Second Thessalonians: Verse by Verse Commentary.* (Santa Barbara: Enduring Word Media, 2013)
13. Guzik, David. *Isaiah: Verse by Verse Commentary.* (Goleta: Enduring Word, 2021)
14. Guzik, David. *James & 1-2 Peter: Verse by Verse Commentary.* (Goleta: Enduring Word Media, 2009)
15. Guzik, David. *Mark: Verse by Verse Commentary.* (Goleta; Enduring Word, 2005)
16. https://www.spurgeon.org/resource-library/sermons/all-at-it/#flipbook/ Accessed 05/08/2023.
17. Joannes, David. *Gospel Privilege.* (Within Reach Global Inc. 2021)

18. Joannes, David. *The Mind of a Missionary: What Global Kingdom Workers Tell Us About Thriving on Mission Today.* (Prescott: Within Reach Global, Inc. 2018)
19. Johnson, Bill. *God is Good: He's Better Than You Think.* (Shippensburg: Destiny Image Publishers, Inc., 2018)
20. Johnson, Christy. *Releasing Prophetic Solutions: Praying Heaven's Promises over Your Home, Family, and Nation.* (Shippensburg: Destiny Image Publishers, 2020)
21. Keller, Timothy. *The Prodigal Prophet: Jonah and the Mystery of God's Mercy.* (New York: Viking, 2018)
22. King, Patricia. *A Prophetic Manifesto for the New Era: 20 Prophetic Words for the 2020s.* (Shippensburg: Destiny Image Publishers, 2020)
23. Kraft, Charles H. Defeating Dark Angels: *Breaking Demonic Oppression in the Believer's Life.* (Bloomington: Chosen Books, 2016)
24. Louis, Peter. *Back to the Gospel: Reviving the Church through the Message that Birthed it.* (Dallas: Braveheart Ministries, Inc, 2017)
25. Maloney, James. *The Dancing Hand of God Volume 1: Unveiling the Fullness of God Through Apostolic Signs, Wonders, and Miracles.* (Bloomington: WestBow Press, 2011)
26. Metaxas, Eric. *Letter to the American Church.* (Washington: Salem Books, 2022)
27. Miskov, Jennifer, Clark, Randy, Engle, Lou. *Fasting for Fire: Igniting Fresh Hunger to Feast upon God.* (Shippensburg: Destiny Image Publishers: 2022)
28. Murillo, Mario. *Vessels of Fire and Glory.* (Shippensburg: Destiny Image Publishers, Inc., 2020)
29. Ortlund, Dane C. Gentle and Lowly: *The Heart of Christ for Sinners and Sufferers.* (Wheaton: Crossway, 2020)
30. Pierce, Mary Jo. *Follow Me: An Unending Conversation with Jesus.* (Southlake: Gateway Press, 2018)
31. Platt, David. *Something Needs to Change: An Urgent Call to Make Your Life Count.* (Colorado Springs: Multnomah, 2019)
32. Randall, Bill. *The Life Jesus Made Possible: Embracing the Kingdom Within our Reach.* (Long Wake: 2018)
33. Rustenbach, Rusty. *A Guide for Listening and Inner-Healing Prayer: Meeting God in the Broken Places.* (Colorado Springs: Nav Press, 2011)
34. Scazzero, Peter. *Emotionally Healthy Spirituality: It's Impossible to Be Spiritually Mature, While Remaining Emotionally Immature.* (Grand Rapids: Zondervan, 2017)
35. Schlink, Basilea. *My All for Him: Fall in Love with Jesus All over Again.* (Bethany House Pub, 2000)

36. Tsarfati, Amir, Yohn, Rick. *Revealing Revelation: How God's Plans for the Future can Change your Life Now.* (Eugene: Harvest House Publishers, 2022)
37. Vallotton, Kris, Johnson, Bill. *The Supernatural Ways of Royalty: Discovering Your Rights and Privileges of Being a Son or Daughter of God.* (Shippensburg: Destiny Image Publishers, 2007)
38. Zodhiates, Spiros. *The Hebrew Greek Key Word Study Bible: NASB-77 Edition.* (Chattanooga: AMG Publishers, 2008)

Made in the USA
Coppell, TX
15 December 2023